Acknowledgments

I'd like to thank first and foremost the otherworldly and invisible companions I have gained during my path and practice who have provided me with endless support and insight not just within my practice but who have also been a shining light in the darkest moments of my life, spirits familiar unto me I thank you and dedicate this book to you. I also want to publicly thank the spirits of Jupiter (as promised) I'd also like to thank my family and friends of all magical walks of life that have played a massive part in my practice over the years My mother Poppy Bowling for teaching me more about the world of spirit, my cousin Susan Hare for always inspiring me and the long calls about our own witchcraft practices, my boyfriend Blair Duncan for constantly supporting me and literally helping me birth this book into being using your Paisley witchcraft! IN NO PARTICULAR ORDER: Ash William Mills without whom without this book wouldn't be made. Thank you for pushing me when times were needed, Jonathan Phoenix-Archer a person with whom ive had the most beautiful experiences with practicing out in the woods in the dark of night whos been a light in times of darkness, Susanne Swanston, Seth David Rodriguez, Ange Simmons, thank you for your companionship all of you. You have all provided incredibly beautiful, life changing experiences to me that I could never have gained with anybody else, thank you. Those experiences I honestly will never forget for the rest of my life and you're all amazing people. Thank you for all being there when times were rough and being a shining light.

For my beautiful Nan Maureen Troubridge, who made me the man I am today. I hope you're proud of me in the world of spirit. Even though you had no interest in folk magic or witchcraft at all, you still paid interest in it for me and supported me every step of the way. I dedicate this book to you just to say thank you for being in my life and generally being an amazing human being.

Barbarous Words

A Compendium of Conjurations, British folk magic, and other popish charms

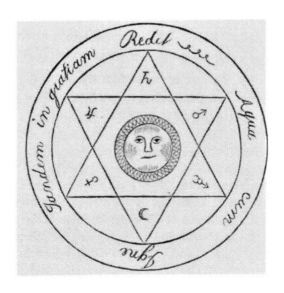

By George Hares

Index

Introduction	9
Devices of the spirit world	47
Benedictions: Healing and charming	85
The sacred heart: Love, favour, and success	103
The Cunning man's arsenal: Defence	123
The Devil's cookbook: curses + maledictions	149
Miscellaneous/all-purpose conjurations	171
Conclusion	201
Bibliography	211

'So how do you conjure up a devil? Music and incantations do they help?'

'If one employs a complete gibberish, just makes a lot of sound, but has intense thought behind it so that you're trying to will over what you want to say, is that you do seem to be able to make contact and to be able to convey your meaning to the spirit force.'

Cecil Williamson 1962 television interview

Introduction

Since the beginning, mankind has always found a way to see the divine within nature and interact with the invisible world petitioning it for expelling or incurring various ailments, bringing forth favours, or desires. Such examples can be seen and found within history all over the world in many different cultures. This ranges from mysterious and ancient idols deposited in a river, peat bodies found in bogs that were given as sacrificial offerings, and even to magnificent and old monuments dotted around the world that stretch back and echo into us the mindset of our ancestors and those who had an impact on the practice and evolution of folk magic and animism. These examples can vary greatly and can be seen all over the world permeating different cultures and countries, radiating even more the connection to the spirit world and the other that humans throughout different periods of time have expressed a great interest towards.

If we look towards Britain as a country and its connection and contribution to folk magic and its regional praxis within history, we can see that Britain over the time has been a very diverse and eclectic mix of practice, taking influence from native cultures such as the Celts, to invading tribes and cultures like the Vikings, romans, and Anglo Saxons, to name a few. There have been many more cultures and practices that have had an impact, but the fact remains that Britain overtime in terms of its folk magic really has become a vast melting pot, leading various different other European cultures to contribute towards its practice. Britain has always been a placed steeped in folklore, mythology, magical practices, and otherworldly activity, leading interest towards this little island that we now know as one of the most influential countries in the world be it for good and be it historically sometimes for bad. The fact remains that Britain has always had a reputation of the otherworldly. Within this book, I want to share with you examples of historical folk magic to examples of modern-day folk magic that can be practiced and utilised. Overall, the aim of this book is to be a manual of folk magic in some way to the modern folk magical practitioner, however that being said it should in no way be seen as fundamental or gospel.

When it comes to personal practice of modern British folk magic, I actively encourage people to go and do their own research here. Do not allow this book to become the only way of practicing present day British folk magic as it is not. The reason I say this is because I do feel sometimes when something is made into a book, it can have a habit of becoming treated as gospel and almost like scripture within itself. I have seen this occur within the magical community at times, and this doesn't necessarily mean it's a reflection of the books or authors themselves that give this impression. The reason I'm mentioning this when it comes to the written word, is because I do feel when something is written, it can be taken and treated as a word for word dogma in a sense and that has never been the idea of this book and its certainly not the style of my personal practice. So please allow your own practice to become part of this book. If there are spells or charms herein that you feel may need adapting or you know you would work better with another ingredient instead of the ingredient given in this book then by all means, I encourage room for creativity. This being said, I would like to also add that the views I have put together in this book do not represent the views of other authors I may have referenced throughout this body of work, they are entirely my own.

Now most of the disclaimers are out the way, I want to mention what this book entails. Most of the spells/charms and incantations within this book are religiously based or what's known as 'popish' meaning roman catholic. That's because cunning folk and witches themselves in Britain were Christian or by the time of the early modern period, had grown up with a Christian mindset and worldview. Because of this, a large collection of charms we have regarding British folk magic make use of the Catholic belief system. Particularly after the reformation in the 1500s as with the religion of Catholicism comes the use of holy waters, rosary beads, petitioning saints, and ancestral veneration which compared to Protestantism, would have been deemed witchcraft and heresy against the crown and state. That is in no way to indicate that Catholicism is plain and simple witchcraft, that is simply not the case. However, some of the attitudes at the time after the reformation, were set towards such a mind frame. Particularly with the rise of Protestantism, and this is something we can see that's evident in the Pendle witch trials of 1612. Where it was mentioned quite frequently by scholars and historians that Catholicism was still prominent in the north of England. Where less focus and attention had been placed rather than the south of England, deeming the north in general to those in the south, a place where those with loose morals and vagabonds were said to live.

After the rise of Protestantism, a lot of Catholics were deemed heretics going against the church of England and prosecuted. Even the various prayers such as the green paternoster, were condemned from head figures of the church such as like bishop Robert Grosseteste. After the reformation, rhymes such as the white paternoster and black paternoster became folk charms. However, it is a subject that you will see arise more in this book regarding the mix of Catholicism and folk magic. With this in mind, and the use of Christian magic throughout this book, I want to add if you feel the need to not work with the Christian elements of British folk magic then it is your personal practice and has nothing to do with me.

This book is based solely off my practice and the practices of some other current day practitioners, that have allowed me to input into here some techniques they used that have all been based off older practices whilst still keeping true to historical elements. Practitioners throughout time have used a myriad of different methods and ways to suit the needs of themselves and their clients. With the idea of this book being a manual of folk charms and conjurations, what is given is a book that holds charms, spells and conjurations used by cunning folk through historical books and grimoires such as: Agrippa's four books of occult philosophy, Reginald Scots Discoverie of Witchcraft, The Magus, The Grimoire of Arthur Gauntlet, Carmina Gadelica, The Cambridge Book of Magic, The Black Dragon, Witchcraft detected and Egyptian secrets or black and white arte for man and beast. Grimoires aside, it is also utilising modern academic research and referencing historical scholars and accounts as well as taking from books of British folk customs and charms from around different areas of the isles. What this book also entails, is modern folk magical remedies in which I as a folk magical practitioner have utilised within my own practice and found effective. I have made a point in merging the Old and New that will become apparent in this book, as I will go into detail in their inspiration and origins.

These new charms and conjurations are contemporary, but they are based off older accounts of British folk magic. How can British folk magic as a tradition carry on if we only think back to what had happened? I'm not asking for spells to strengthen the Wi-Fi connection, (however at times it would be amazing if such a conjuration existed!) of course, by asking this question, it's not to dispute the past and the information we have now, as the information and references we have are all extremely important and without them there wouldn't be this current of folk magic existing now. How can we expect the tradition of folk magic to carry on if we only use folk magic from past environments? It is within my own opinion, that in order to move forward we need to suit folk magic to ourselves and our environment we have around us in the NOW. What's the point of performing a travelling charm from the Carmina Gadelica, if it isn't relevant to our surroundings we have now? If we live in a city where there aren't corries and valleys and forests and were travelling to a city break abroad, then it's not relevant. Don't be afraid to change charms to where you are now and suited to the environment, you're in. Know where the workings are from out of respect for the academics, scholars, magicians, folk tales, and cunning folk that have supplied them. As by doing so they've helped immortalise British folk magic rather than it is becoming a distant memory of the past. In my opinion, it must suit your actual situation you're conjuring for. I have made travelling charms for loved ones that have been based off older practices but suited to more current ways, such as using a thread of hag stones and keys and speaking to each item for each step of their journey. For example, each time I've knotted in an item I've made a statement:

> *"Protect them whilst they are flying back and forth to the city of Paris, In the name of land sky and sea fiat."*

> **Next Knot**: *"Protect them in the city of Paris against all evil spirits, evil men and evil deeds in the name of land sky and sea fiat."*

> **Next knot**: *"Protect them against all acts of accidents, terrorism and acts of violence in the name of land sky and sea fiat".*

You get the idea of it by now, I'm sure. Each knot was made relevant to their unique situation, which folk magic should be suited to. This is just an example of older forms of magic being applied to the modern world, but I hope the example itself gives an outline as to what this book is trying to achieve, to give inspiration to others for making folk magic more of a living tradition in the present and suited to the needs of the NOW. Still going with the idea of travelling charms, another example can be taken from Alexander Carmichaels book the Carmina Gadelica written in 1901 as mentioned above which contains hymns, prayers and incantations collected from the western isles of Scotland. If we work the following prayer that was sung by a pilgrim before undergoing a pilgrimage along with his family and friends as the journey began in which it goes as such:

"Life be in my speech, sense in what I saw, The bloom of cherries on my lips, Till I come back again, The love Christ Jesus gave be filling every heart for me, The love Christ Jesus gave filling me for everyone. Traversing corries, traversing forests, traversing valleys long and wild, the fair white Mary still uphold me, The sheapeard Jesu be my shield, The fair white Mary still uphold me , the sheapeard jesu be my shield. "

An absolutely gorgeous and beautiful prayer, but how relevant would it be the modern-day practitioner now? As mentioned, how many corries do we pass through and valleys long and wild? Normally when we go travelling a lot of the time it will be overseas, so we need to make it actually relevant to what we are doing. There's no point reciting an old travelling charm if it doesn't have relevance to our environment around us. Of course, if we are passing corries and valleys long and wild then utilise this charm intact. However, for the traveller nowadays, I feel this may be more relevant:

"Life be in my speech, sense in what I saw, The bloom of cherries on my lips, Till I come back again, The love Christ Jesus gave be filling every heart for me, The love Christ Jesus gave filling me for everyone. Traversing roads, traversing airports, Traversing Sky in planes, traversing Cities, traversing nature, the fair white Mary still uphold me, The Shepheard Jesu be my shield, The fair white Mary still uphold me, the Shepheard jesu be my shield."

By doing this, we can do our own research and apply it to the now and keep folk magic as a living tradition that carries on and survives. We have this idea of a red thread particularly in modern witchcraft traditions, stretching on through different eras of time going back and connecting us to other practitioners through oral lore passed down and given to each person.

Unfortunately, in modern day Britain, this is not the case at all. Lore has been lost through mass industrialisation, mass capitalism, ignorance and not wanting to keep those traditions alive seeing them as 'merely superstition'. There are of course still to this day, folk charms and remedies passed down to various families. My family on my dad's side has a wart charm that involves rubbing a wart onto a piece of ham, then flushing it down the toilet and not telling anybody. My sister used this, as well as a cleaner in a previous workplace and both troublesome warts rotted and went away. Trust my family to head for the toilet duck when things go wrong! The point of this is, there isn't an unbroken thread of oral lore of an entire tradition of British Folk Magic passed from one person to another that goes through generation to generation. There is however a red thread of knowledge that we now have through historical accounts, items, and research, we have access to knowledge now at the touch of our fingertips.

I want to further add from this point, that this book isn't claiming the newer charms given through inspiration of the old isn't indicating that by utilising these newer charms, you're working the exact magic of the cunning folk from the early modern period. It's just trying to keep the survival of British folk magic through an adaptable and contemporary working scope. Perhaps the thread mentioned above is still there, but it only remains red through the knowledge. The knowledge we have isn't broken. It's still passed down and we have access to that via academic resources and lore combined, so instead of a red thread that goes on for eons it's a red thread of knowledge that we all have access to and that we can all grab hold of.

When it comes to the main practices within folk magic in Britain, they aren't always necessarily just always reserved at cunning folk practices. For there existed another form of folk magic known as witchcraft which to the rest of society and particularly to cunning folk in the early modern period, had a darker and more sinister path, which we will tackle in the next two sections. In recent years, we have seen a very big rise and revival in the modern-day praxis of folk magic, and I can only hope that as a practitioner, this book helps carry that on and reconnect people to the more simplistic but effective practices of folk magic of Britain. Going back to the idea of Britain being a melting pot of various countries and cultures throughout the years. I have also included within this book, a handful of examples of folk magic from other parts of Europe in general and I hope this gives an example of other European folk magic having some ties and influences together.

Cunning Folk

Throughout the early modern period to the early 1900s within Britain there were those that were known as cunning folk, white Witches, Conjurers, wisemen/women, faith healers, pellars, fairy doctors, the list of terminology goes on depending on what area of Britain you ventured to and what area in the magical arts focused. These people were seen to be Magical practitioners of their time, and often were seen as consultants to the spirit world typically acting as mediators and asking or petitioning spirits for assistance with the so many struggles which others and themselves faced daily. There is a distinction between the cunning folk and the witches in terms of their roles in society and their intentions, which shall be explained in due time. However, regarding the practices of cunning folk, let's look at their roles within society and what some of their practices actively entailed. The

services provided by cunning folk or 'white witches' could vary dramatically from minor charming such as ridding people of warts, bone setting, charming burns, to full unbewitching services which involved the sending back of the evil eye, witchcraft or maleficia.

This radiates even more the mind frame people had as In the older times, things were very different from now. The fear of illness and crippling diseases lurked around every corner, food supplies could be short due to crops failing or cattle dying, if you lost an animal to disease, it meant your family could starve to death, and not only that, but things in general held more value than they statistically do in today's world where things are so readily available but yet so disposable. It is obvious that finding lost items in general was also heavily popular and could literally be life or death for a lot of people. The methods used for finding lost objects could again greatly range, from summoning planetary/angelic intelligences or familiar spirits, to more simple methods by burning an old shoe with dirt contained within gathered from a crossroads whilst reciting the apostle's creed in Latin.

    Love was a service demanded by clients and always has been in a sense this hasn't particularly changed amongst many different practices of folk magic and witchcraft around the world. Many people wanted to know who they would marry, and frequently would perform divination on various nights such as midsummer or St Johns eve, to find out who their future spouses would be. Alternatively, things would get very hands on, and cunning folk would be consulted to bewitch the other person in question, making them crave and desire the client's attention and favour.

    Cunning folk would mostly serve their local community acting as spiritual consultants, but also supplying magical services as well as sometimes acting as medical doctors. Interestingly, it wasn't unheard of for those from other counties to journey and consult cunning folk through their reputation they upheld from stories told from their many clients by word of mouth, as their successes would spread far beyond and travel wide. For instance, Essex cunning man James Cunning Murrell also known as 'The Devils master' had clients that would travel from other counties outside of Essex, because they had heard about his abilities and his famous Iron witch bottles he had fashioned from the local blacksmith for a shilling.

    From the early modern period, the fear of witches and the evil eye as it is known was prominent and was even evident. These beliefs (though admittedly were less popular compared to the early modern period) still held power in the Victorian era to the early nineteen-hundreds, such is the time of James Cunning Murrell. If one neighbour had fell out with another and their cattle had become sick, it would have raised a lot of suspicions around the person they had an argument with. Even more particularly, if a threat followed by a misfortune which was said or mentioned by the opposing party. Normally afterwards, that's when divination and unbewitching services would be needed and the local cunning man or wisewomen would step in. However, there were also other ways that would kill two birds with one stone in a sense that would not only lift the curse, but at the same time also identify the suspected witch. The most famous out of a list of these myriad of methods within folk magic were known as witch bottles. These apotropaic devices would normally represent the witches or ill-wisher's bladder and then would typically be filled with the patient's hair, nails, broken glass, broken mirror, and pins or iron nails that would be typically bent to 'send back' the evil eye. It would then be filled with the patient's urine, corked tight, and then put onto a blazing fire. The idea was that as the urine heated up, so did the bladder of the witch. It was thought that due to the sympathetic nature of the magical act, that the witch would also suffer as there held a belief that the witch and the patient were linked together through their curse by blood and other bodily fluids. It was seen as something that left an imprint and link of the suspected witch to the victim. In many cases, the belief would be that the next day or sometime after the charm had been worked, that the suspected witch would then present themselves to the house of the one who was ill wished. This would involve the witch normally looking rather uncomfortable and asking to borrow something from the person who had been bewitched. The general idea when such an event occurred, was to refuse the witch any help or items she wanted to borrow. Sometimes the bottle itself wasn't burnt but buried within or by the persons threshold. This act was performed so that it came into contact regularly with the person who made the bottle thus also acting as a decoy, directing any maleficia sent to the bottle rather than the person themself.

There are also examples of witch bottles being deposited in riverbeds. According to a talk at the hidden charms conference two by Dr Peter Hewitt, the collections researcher and museum manager of the museum of witchcraft in Boscastle. During this talk Peter Hewitt explained there were 2 bottles found by a road in Stockport which contained dragons' blood, urine, and pins. Many claimed that it was used by fortune tellers to bewitch lover's unfaithful partners, other witnesses claimed it was used by witches to curse their enemies. In the end a wise woman was consulted, and she had suggested this discovered bottle was to be broken by a running stream by a south flowing river. The idea that running water had the power to cleanse and purge these bottles from having their hold and influence over others, which you will see evident throughout this book. One witness then also went on to tell another story about a witch bottle that was buried in the bed of the river Mersey, underneath the wellington bridge arch by a witch. A river, that I am thankful to have had the privilege to be more than familiar within my own personal magical practice. A wise woman was again consulted, and the bewitched woman was told to stand in the same spot by a river for a given time, as several spirits were said to pass her until one came and was dismissed alongside the ailments, by the planet ruler after she had addressed herself.

Once again, the use of water arises here as a means to wash away the afflictions. In particular, a south flowing river. In rowan tree and red thread written by Thomas Davidson, it is mentioned that in 1631, a man named John Mill in Tweedmouth was accused of witchcraft and was alleged to have" made a man's wife wash her husband's shirt in south running water and then put it on him; whereupon he recovered" by means to disperse of an illness or ill wishing that would befall the client. In terms of counteracting or turning around malevolent magic however, witch bottles and rivers weren't the only tools utilised. There were many other ways one could turn back and send back a curse which will be listed in due time within this book. The services provided by cunning folk also involved Finding and detecting thieves, including retrieving back stolen items these would all fall within the wise persons realm.

There are also some conjurations and charms from cunning folk that in some ways crossed over into the realms of cursing. These charms were to typically either to do harm back to a witch and counteract their maledictions or to inflict pain onto a thief which would force the thief compelling them to return the stolen goods through various methods of magical acts and incantations. One of the charms within this book, which is a charm to spoil a thief, a witch, or any other enemy taken from Reginald Scots discoverie of witchcraft, involves the use of cutting a Hazel wand "in the name of the person you mean to beat or maim" and calling upon the holy trinity to punish the thief or witch. This in some ways would appear like more of a curse upon the thief and in that sense can leave very blurred boundaries between the idea of sending forth maledictions and cursing or what's also known in east Anglia as 'Tudding'. The terminology of tudding coming from the idea of the toad being a creature favoured by witches and sometimes being a disguise for the Devil himself. The toad the being thought of as a creature bearing the powers to send the evil eye. It was also though that the toad was an animal that appeared onto the devil's coat of arms. The terminology of witch has changed depending on the time scale we look into. For instance, to have been called a witch in the early modern period would not have been a good thing at all compared to those who were known as village witches, wayside witches and especially the popular term: 'white witch' in the early 1900s. During this period, the use and terminology of the term 'witch' changed massively compared to the meaning of witch in the seventeenth century and prior. This further adds onto the cunning folk/witchcraft crossover, and it is not only seen with its terminologies but also its practitioners throughout the ages. Another example is, George Pickingill who resided in Canewdon, Essex from 1816 to 1909. It is told he was sought for over the county and beyond for his ability which varied in varieties be it from curing cattle, charming ailments, and controlling the witches who were doing harm to his clients. These all seem areas that would put somebody into the brackets of cunning folk, however on the flip side of the argument, Pickingil also threatened people with curses and would quite often be found drunk in a hedge on harvest day. The reason being, it was said he used to threaten the farmers that if they didn't pay him beer, he would bewitch all the machinery. George Pickingill also claimed to have control over 9 witch covens in Essex. Although to be entirely fair, I will also input that George Pickingill at one point by newspapers had also labelled himself as Britain's oldest man and this eventually turned out to be untrue. He also on one hand told people he had 9 imps in the ways of mice that would do his work for him in the fields all day whilst he sat back, smoked his pipe and they done all the work! A colourful character nevertheless!

A large concept that British folk magic and witchcraft share in general, is animism. The belief that every tree, rock, river, and every living being has a soul and spirit and that through this concept, we can commune with those spirits and energies utilising their assistance normally in exchange for offerings or favours via pacts. Animistic practice is something that is not new and can be seen all over the world in different cultures throughout different time periods and even in the modern world it still remains. Animism is ancient and one only needs to see the practices of British folk magic and folk customs in general to see that it played a major part in people's lives and once was integral to the lives and practice of the common folk.

With the crossover of cunning folk and witches, you could perhaps argue that because the cunning person was working and utilising the powers of God rather than the Devil, it made an exemption to the ill wishes being sent out. For their skills and having the ability to influence the community around them, cunning folk would also have gathered reputations in the community mentioned earlier. So, it comes to no surprise that they would also be feared by the local community to some extent. Due to these reputations upheld, stories and word of mouth would have demonstrated to others just the amount of power they weld over the mundane world.

It was also cunning folk that were sometimes involved in witch trials being the ones that were consulted to find out the accused witch, to stand in trial and testify against the accused witch. In some unfortunate cases, actually being the suspected witch themselves through charming or spells that had gone awry with clients. An example of this for instance, would be the cunning folk being asked to heal a sick person and the person taking an unfortunate turn for the worse and dying. This to some at the time, could be seen as the wise person themselves being seen as a catalyst for inflicting that maleficia through their otherworldly connections. The reason being the charms they had worked had not taken any effect and had in fact suffered mishap or death to the clients' cattle or loved ones involved. In terms of the law and the way it saw those that were involved in the arts magical, at a certain period particularly within the era of King James, there would have been this attitude that saw no difference between the role of the cunning folk and the witch as they would have been seen as the same thing such as mentioned in a dialogue within King James Daemonologie:

'what forme of punishment thinke ye merites these magicians and witches? For I see that ye account them to be all alike guiltie? They ought to be put to death according to the law of God, the civil and imperiall law, and municipall law of all Christian nations.'

Another frequent practice among cunning folk involved the practice of divination, in which the wise person would be consulted to find out various answers to questions that the client wanted to know.

This was achieved by many various methods, one of the most common was through means of scrying where the client would be instructed to scry into a reflective image so that it would be the client themselves that saw the person who would be responsible for answers to questions typically relating to theft or witchcraft, but would also stretch to other areas. For the operation of divination, many different items were utilised and worked for this purpose such as a mirror, a vessel of water, or in some cases the urine of the bewitched person/animal again reiterating the idea that the witch and victim is inheritably linked by the spell or conjuration that was cast against them. In 1876 a woman named Emma Foot gave some of her sick mother's urine to a cunning man named Frederick Culliford and asked if there had been any ill wishing involved in her mother's demise. The cunning man took the bottle of her mother's urine, shook it, and looked at it whilst confirming there had indeed been witchcraft afoot. Forms of divination weren't just restricted to urine gazing or scrying within the practices of British folk magic. A well-known method within popular magic, was performed from the art of heating up lead, known as Molybdomancy. The most common praxis amongst wise persons would involve dropping it through a keyhole into a vessel of water and reading the images given. Sometimes the wise women or wise man were also known to be in some ways a prophet or a seer. Possessing the ability to be able to peer into the otherworld or the future, or thereby gaining information from familiar spirits and other spiritual allies, about certain situations. Another famous method of divination that would be famous with finding out thieves, would be using a bible and key or the sieve and shears method where the objects would be balanced between two people, whilst names of the suspected would be recited. When the objects such as the bible dropped, or the sieve turned at the name recited, they would indicate who the perpetrator was. There were many cunning folks throughout the ages, so their methods differed in terms of divination, and this is something to be mindful of here. Not in Britain, but in the republic of Ireland, Biddy Early would read for her clients with a blue bottle, comparing this to Cunning Murrell with his iron goggles that were able to see into the future shows vast difference in practice. The way one cunning man would have practiced, would have been different to the way another cunning person would have worked. Of course, their methods would have been similar and ran alongside the tradition of cunning folk magic, but there would have been different ways people worked.

Naturally this doesn't just stop at divination, it involves other aspects of the conjurers practice, much like folk magicians in other parts of the world. Other popular areas the conjurer focused upon was healing, again this could have been from simple charming such as ridding earache, ridding headaches to ridding fevers or what was known as the 'Ague' which covered not just fevers but also chills. Other methods of healing would involve the use of natural/holy springs or wells which would typically carry the patronage of a saint or have spiritual bodies tied to them through various parts of folklore and oral legend from the land. The conjurer would go to these places, alone or sometimes with their clients, and would interact with the spirit force, calling for assistance and aid yet again acting as the person that communes between the world of the visible and invisible. Well water would be sprinkled upon the ill person along with an incantation in charming away the ailment the person was suffering. When it comes to healing magical practices, their practices could again vary greatly. From knotting cord for sprains which we will go into later in this book, to taking a person's clothing and immersing it in the well water and hanging it upon a tree.

27

The latter practice mentioned, being the famous 'clootie charm'.

Other aspects were more simplistic in nature, when a cunning person would cut off a piece of hazel and use it for their wand whilst also muttering barbarous words to heal cattle this was another large aspect and spiritual interest the cunning folk held as again these were very important parts of practice and there are still charmers today within rural Britain, that are called upon to help heal cattle in rural agricultural communities.

The Witch

As well as the idea of the cunning man and his ways, there also existed a more notorious and sinister counterpart of folk magical practice: witchcraft. This practice was seen very differently in comparison to modern forms of witchcraft we have today. The name witchcraft in the early modern period to many people conjured up dark and sinister images that ensnared the human condition literally bringing the fear of God (or in fact the very opposite) into people's hearts. The witch was a person that by cunning folk and the community, would have been seen as a direct threat and would have been seen almost as a spiritual infection within the community inflicting damage and suffering through the power of evil wherever they went. It was part of the cunning folk's job to detect this practice and undo the harm that had been done via means of counteractive folk magic. The witch would have been typically seen in the early modern period, as a person that had made a contract with the Devil himself typically involving selling their soul in exchange for supernatural powers and a familiar spirit that would be gifted to the witch after their renunciation of their baptism and their pledge was made to Satan.

There are also some interesting ideas involving the witch having blurred crossovers and lined between the idea of the physical and corporeal. For instance, a good example of this is mentioned in a verse in the Lancashire folk song Old Pendle:

"*When witches do fly on a cold winter's night, We won't tell a soul and we'll bolt the door tight, We'll sit by the fire and keep ourselves warm, Until once again we are safe in your arms.*"

Other examples of this can be seen within the idea of shapeshifting told in folk tales that speak of witches taking form as a hare, menacing hunters, and creating havoc amongst the community. When the mysterious animal is finally shot or injured within the fable told and disappears, the suspected witch is seen to have also contracted the exact physical injuries the creature incurred. This really Bridges the relationship to the witches' fetch (their spirit) and their body as their familiars and in some modern forms of traditional witchcraft practices and paths this idea can really intermingle. Another further point to this blurred crossover betwixt the physical and the spiritual, is that there are beliefs in folklore that see the tree Elder as inhabiting an old woman or a witch. There is also another folk belief that witches themselves can hide in the elder tree which once again further reiterates the idea of the witch herself being betwixt physical and spiritual.

In many very clear-cut ways, the role of the witch and cunning folk were very different but also similarities ensued between them. Essentially, the role of the cunning person was to bring benefit onto the community such as healing or the return of lost items, whereas the role of the witch herself was to inflict damage onto society and ensure harm came to those around them. The ways of harm varied and could involve a numerous number of aspects from spoiling milk or beer, butter failing to churn, cursing and harming people or cattle, causing harvests to fail, etc. The idea of the fairy worlds and the good folk would have also played both a very important role. For both cunning folk and witches also, there are many witch trials and accounts that speak of the suspected witch journeying to the otherworld to meet their faery counterparts and gaining knowledge from the invisible world and bringing that information back to the mundane. An example of this is found in the case of accused witch Bessie Dunlop, who claimed her familiar spirit Tom Reid would take her by the apron and would have had her go with him to Elphame. This similarity carries with it elements that can be found within aspects of shamanism around various parts of the world. The idea of the one who walks separately aside from everybody else who is in direct contact with the spirit world, being able to walk in between this world and the world of the invisible.

If we look at the lore of the witch; rubbing their bodies with flying ointment made with entheogenic herbs especially harvested and made for the purpose of soul flight. A person who is able to fly across the sky naked, holding onto a steed whether that be a broom, an animal, or an accompanying familiar spirit, which went with them into the night sky to meet with various entities such as the Devil, Faery folk, or other spirits. The witch being an entity having the ability to cross into the other worlds to gain information on charms and spells. It's evident these elements and ideas of the witch does indicate aspects of shamanic practice. The idea being that the shaman is a person who walks between the worlds and stands upon the very edge of society such as the witch and the cunning folk. The difference being that cunning folk were seen as being a valuable part of the community with their uses, whereas the witch most of the time would have been seen as an active threat. Through journeying to the otherworld, this person is able to bring the 'medicine' or information of charms and spells back to the mundane world (the medicine being seen as the 'physik' the cure, given in a physical or spiritual manner to the patient by cunning folk and the information being the charms given to the witches and cunning folk supplied by spirit allies.) I will point out though, whilst on the matter that witchcraft isn't shamanism. It just carries elements in it of shamanic practice. There is a huge difference. Emma Wilby in her fantastic book cunning folk and familiar spirits, draws impressive similarities between these shamanic practices whilst also making points to differentiate the opposing Familiars between the two variations of folk magician. The cunning folk working with the Fairy familiar, and the witch working with the Demonic Familiar.

Does this mean that witchcraft in its practice way back when or today is inherently evil? No. I'm just trying to give the mindset and worldview that most folks had at the time. Witches were seen as those who were different or who had been ostracised from the community, they were seen as complete outsiders that didn't fit into societal norms. How many times do we see those in this day-and-age who are completely misunderstood and tend to walk on the outskirts of society rather than fully playing a part? This is something I've also felt within myself and I'm sure many other practitioners have themselves. However, despite all of this, I'm still an active member of society and most people that are misunderstood still play an active part within society. Where as in the early modern period, if you were accused of being a witch or in league with the devil, you were at the most part shunned from the rest of society which would have realistically had a much more bigger impact upon a person other than them 'feeling different' or never fitting in.

Let's also be realistic here, that witchcraft is a difficult one historically to pinpoint what people were actually doing and honestly in most cases, if anything at all. As a lot of the testimonials we have, have been confessions from people who were interrogated, tortured, exposed to harsh living conditions through incarceration, or blackmailed and who would have said anything to spare a single moment out of that pain. There is also the fact that the witch became a scape goat in a brutal world mentioned earlier in the introduction of sickness creeping around every corner, unpredictability, and many other factors that contributed to the hardship many faced living in the early modern period. For all the wrong doings in the village, for all that had gone awry within the community, the witch was the one who was responsible for it rather than basic factors, like sanitary living conditions, exhaustion through over working, basic medical factors with no advancements what we have today.

However, there are parts of confessions that do hold similarities. The idea of going to the sabbat and making pacts with the devil and communing with spirits or the good folk in other worlds and invisible realm. We can also see various confessions where we can once again still see that element and crossover of Christianity and paganism playing its part and having influence here. The Scottish accused witch Andro Man claimed that the Queen of Elphame's consort was known as Christ-Sunday, who was a stag and who would emerge from a hill out of the snow. It is my own personal speculation that witchcraft at that time if it did exist as a practice, was made up of animism, luciferianism, the faery faith, and Christianity. Of course, I think it's impossible for one to say for definite and my speculations are merely speculation rather than fact itself, so bare this in mind. However, there are many elements of these crossovers in witchcraft trials and confessions that have made me come to that conclusion.

You may have noticed a pattern when speaking about cunning folk and witches, they tend to intermingle and ive drawn comparisons between them. Of course, as mentioned I am not stating they are the same entity absolute. Given the factors I have given such a statement is ludicrous. However, when it comes to applying modern practice, I see myself as both. For instance, when I'm working magic of healing for a client or a sick person, I am what is known as 'the white witch' working beneficial healing to those in need and I am practicing British folk magic. However, when I am working more sinister magic to somebody who has wronged me or others, in that moment I become 'the black witch' and am very much within the realms of witchcraft. Admittedly I don't use these following terms very much, but the two opposing practices blend into my practice yet remain apart. Many people will often ask me the question: what are you? A white witch or a black witch? My answer? Yes. I am literally both, to me it doesn't matter what kind of witch you are, it matters if you're a good person or not.

Folk Catholicism

"Cunning folk used religious substances and artefacts for healing purposes: Holy water, Eucharist wafers (sneaked out of church after communion) candle wax, scrapings from religious statues, and water from holy wells were all employed outside the perimeters of official church usage"

Emma Wilby: Cunningfolk and familiar spirits.

Now we get to the part that can leave a real bitter taste in people's mouths, particularly when it comes to certain members of the pagan community. However, I cannot sit here and tell you different because the alternative does not exist. There is no actual evidence and accounts from the early modern period of Cunning folk being involved in a secret underground pre-Christian pagan religion. There... I said it. This idea was brought forward largely by a body of anthropologists in the Victorian era, when at the time a lot of romanticism was created when looking at the older pre-Christian religions and cults. One prominent figure during this time who played a key part was known as Margaret Murray, who wrote her book God of the witches in 1933. The book gives the idea that witches and cunning folk were practicing a secret underground religion, in which various historians and scholars such as Owen Davies and Ronald Hutton have actively discredited time and time again. Owen Davies in his book Popular magic: cunning folk in English history states the following:

"This leads us back in a roundabout way to the applicability of the term pagan to cunning folk. The origins and exact meaning of the word are problematic, and this is not the place to debate them. But in reference to Europe it can be uncontroversially used to describe the Pre-Christian worship of multiple Gods and spirits. By the medieval period the church may not have obliterated all signs of pre-Christian beliefs and practices in England, but it had effectively suppressed all vestiges of paganism as a religion and a mode of worship."

The idea of a secret underground pagan cult needs to be scrapped in my eyes if we are to respect actual history and  also the legacy that cunning folk and practitioners of British folk magic have left behind. Myself and other authors over the years have been attacked for supplying this information by some neopagans that think differently, and I've even been spoken out against presenting this fact after I had spoken at a talk involving the fact cunning folk were Christian. The person had stated that this was a very 'British' idea in thinking this and that in fact, other historians and scholars around the world

35

think differently in regard to British cunning folk and their religious beliefs. I am yet to find any written evidence that supplies this hypothesis, and the person did not give any valid references at all, further adding less confidence in their remarks. There are also authors that have been attacked due to their books written on folk magic, that involve the use of Christian orientated charms. This is extremely distasteful, by keeping that mindset and doing this you are actively denying historical accuracy.

Do I think that pagan elements had died out completely? Not at all. In fact, we can see that folk magic incorporates the use of pagan elements heavily. For instance, the use of calling forth the holy trinity to dispel what was known as elf shot. The belief that the fae or good folk could shoot arrows to people/cattle and render them with illness and bad health. This crossover of Christianity and pagan elements still lies within our folk magic, as is evident from the following charm involving the use of the holy trinity, Odin and Loki:

The following charm from Lincolnshire used to take away the ague, via the use of horseshoes. Three horseshoes would be nailed to the affected persons bed post, then the hammer used was placed crossways over them. The charmer then took the hammer with the left hand, tapped each horseshoe with it and then said:

Father, Son, and the Holy Ghost
Nail the Devil to the post.
Thrice I strike with holy crook,
One for God, one for Wod, and one for Lok.

Other aspects of Christianity and pagan elements combining in British folk magic, would be the use of wells or springs within charming. There are mentions of the ancient people of pre-Christian Britain worshipping at wells or bodies of water, including votive offerings given to sacred springs or vessels of water. One of the most well-known charms being mentioned earlier, the famed clootie charm. Where an item of the ill persons clothing is taken to the holy well, dipped within the water, and hung up upon a nearby tree.

As a side note, I will actually mention that in these times we have to be mindful of the damage this charm can actually create to the environment around us including its wildlife. I have seen clootie charms that were made of material that could not biodegrade such as synthetic ribbon, elastic bands, and even somebody's bra strap! I digress back to the original subject, but I do feel this has to be noted down.

The fact cunning folk were Christian or utilised Christian symbology within their practice, doesn't necessarily mean that they actually fell within the realms of acceptance within the church itself. The methods and ways they utilised religious paraphernalia and charms would have to most Christians not been acceptable. There are also examples of witches or cunning folk making use of rosary beads within their charming methods such as Mother Didge of Kershall, who would use rosary beads and candle wax in order to cure burns and what was knowns as St anthonys fire. This was also known as ergotism which was caused by a fungus that infects rye and other cereals, causing people to hallucinate, and has been mentioned by some historians as a potential doorway that was opened to create the witch craze in early modern Europe and in the new worlds.

Another example of the separation concerning God of the church and cunning folk in general, is an account of Derbyshire Cunning woman Elizabeth Wright. Who in an account of her unbewitching cattle, the following was said: 'She came to the mans house, knelt down before the cow, crossed her with a stick in the forehand, and prayed to her God, since which time the cow continued well.'

As Joyce Froome points out in her book wicked enchantments, there were distinguished differences most people felt in their God compared to the God of the cunning folk. This also points to people believing the God of the cunning folk in some cases was the Devil, as cunning folk werent seen as following the God of the religion that had influence over the main governing body of the country at the time. An example of this found within charms, can also be seen in the book Orkney and Shetland islands by George F Black. What's given, is a curious Scottish verbal benediction known as forespoken waters which is aimed at saining water for magical uses of healing humans or cattle. The use of language here is interesting, displaying a dual aspect of benevolent and sinistral influences of the God petitioned:

"In the name of him that can cure and kill, This water shall cure all earthly ill Shall cure the blood and flesh and bone For ilka ane there is a stone May she fleg all trouble, sickness, pain. Cure without and cure within Cure the heart, the horne, the sin."

The practice of this mix of Catholicism and magic was

seen as blasphemy especially at the times of the reformation when Protestantism took over England. As being catholic during the reformation, was deemed heresy against the crown and country itself. Even Reginald Scot who wrote his famous book *a discoverie of witchcraft* believed that the act of transubstantiation within mass, the moment where the wine and bread becomes the physical flesh and blood of Christ was in itself an act of sorcery. So rather have been a confirmed Christianity among cunning folk, the ways these were utilised radiated morely the idea of folk Catholicism. For instance, let's take a branch of folk Catholicism such as certain saints in Mexico such as Santa Muerte; a Mexican folk saint of death that the catholic church has not canonised as an official saint, and has spoken out against.

This is the most obvious in terms of folk Catholicism as Mexico has a rich heritage and culture in terms of brujeria and folk Catholicism, and quite often they tend to blur. Now Mexico is a very different country from Britain altogether, and so I am not in any way drawing up similarities between the two countries culture and heritage. I am merely pointing out there is a similarity regarding the aspect of folk magic and Christianity here and how acceptable they are to the church itself. There is a huge difference between Christianity and the church. The church is the body of power that gives dogmatic orders and has control. Where-as Christianity or another religion can be expressed by an individual in the ways that suit them and to their personal experiences they have with it. A person only needs to think of the various branches of Christianity that have emerged to understand this, ranging from the liberal to the damn right extreme and ugly. There are many Catholics I know of that have faith, but do not respect the church whilst also practicing their religion at the same time.

However, let me make it clear and also point out that not all wise people were catholic. In the case of James Cunning Murrell, he was baptised in St Mary the Virgin Church in Hawkwell which is a protestant church. What's normally not found within a structure of dogmatic Catholicism, is the easy transition from heaven to hell when it comes to employing various powers for help in the mundane world. There seems to also exist within folk magic the mix up between the ethereal and the infernal powers and it is not uncommon for folk practitioners to utilise what works. For instance, there is a spell in this book in order to transfer an illness which involves calling on the aid of the devil. This isn't just subjected to the spell mentioned, it becomes a regular occurrence throughout history and in fact even has influence over some well-known figures from the early modern period that have had influence on British folk magic. A really well-known spell but a good example of this which indicates this phenomenon, is from accused witch Isobel Gowdie and her charm to transform into a hare:

"I shall go into a hare, with sorrow and sych and mickle care and I shall go in the devils name ay while I come home again."

And to change back the following would be stated:

"hare hare god send thee care I am in a hares likeness now but I shall be in a woman likeness even now"

It is obvious from this charm that to somebody like

Isobel, the ability to change into a hare fell into the realms of the devil whilst the ability to change back came under the dominion of God himself. One could further speculate that perhaps to those in the early modern period, the realms of the wild fell under the devil and his demise. Whilst the realm of humans fell beneath God's glory. However, at this point it is only speculation, but an interesting point made in all.

I want to end this section by addressing that I am in no way hating on modern practicing pagan traditions or pagans at all. In fact, I have so many people in my life that are pagan and mean so much to me. I have so much respect for paganism, I just think there has been a non-existent rumour of this going around for some time now when it comes to cunning folk and paganism, and I think it's important to honour history as it is rather than alter it towards our suiting. You don't have to do the spells or charms in this book based on popish practice, they can be altered and made to your own religious or spiritual suitings. Its just important to know where these charms come from and to know the true history of cunning folk from early modern Britain.

Making use of what we have around us

In a lot of modern witchcraft traditions, (including modern traditional witchcraft) there tends to be the use of many different tools which are used for a myriad of specific purposes within folk magical operation. These tools tend to be put aside and fit only for the purpose in which they were made, never to stray away from their original purpose. Within British folk magic, if we look at

41

its practice throughout history, a large portion of the time, it makes use of what we ourselves have around us and to hand. Once again radiating the simplicity and practicality of Folk Magic in general.

A person need only look back into old remedies or charms to see that it makes use of what you have around you, rather than tools set out and made for that particular purpose. For instance, my broom I have can be used for sweeping out/in negative/positive energies, but it is also a broom and that's exactly what it does Sweep! I'm not shy of using the tools I have for their actual purpose, and this certainly would have been the case if we go back to the early modern period. People wouldn't have had the money to afford a separate working knife only fit for cutting herbs, they used what they had around them. I can only speak of how I work, and how I know other folk practitioners to work. Again, I understand everyone is different here and so please be aware I am not in any way speaking on behalf of ALL folk magicians. Such a statement in itself is Ludacris but to me, if something already has those properties such as the broom, to use it for what it was made for means you're strengthening those virtues and properties that broom holds, thus adding more potency into your workings. To me, to use a broom for sweeping is to keep those powers of being able to sweep intentions or incantations to and fro because when it comes to dirt, that is literally what it does! So why is it only limited to sweeping dust and dirt? What better way than to work practically than this.

  I have a working knife and I also have a wand, however that hasn't stopped me not taking the wand to a working site, and grabbing a stick from the ground, working with it during that spell I am doing. It also hasn't stopped me using my knife to cut herbs, but also flip burgers after a post ritual BBQ! I have a cup that I use for serving the spirits but il also not think twice about drinking from it, if its good enough for me it's good enough for the spirits. Many people would be shocked at this, but to me the spiritual and the physical are intertwined massively. I feel that using these tools in such a manner radiates that idea and by once again using them for what they are designed for, only strengthens their virtues rather than weakens it. It is a reminder the world of spirits and men are in fact, intertwined.

Starting new traditions.

When it comes to your magic, like above do not be afraid to utilise and employ that which is around you. Some of the most potent and powerful spells ive worked have been created by the spur of the moment, utilising what I have around me and listening to the spirits. I have done many a working where a 'happy accident' has occurred. If I'm outside working a charm or a conjuration and something presents itself to me and I feel a pull towards it, I'll employ it in my working! It's not been unknown for things to drop onto the working too when working outside, such as a piece of oak and at that point ive thought to myself: "Oak to strengthen, thankyou spirits." Likewise, when indoors sometimes the odd bottle of holy water or well water has fallen over and some of the water has been absorbed in the charm. To me, that means the spirits or allies I'm working with and have called for that to become incorporated within the working. As mentioned, I have had very successful spell casting with my statement of intentions and working with what I had around me at that time. In my opinion, old style magic doesn't just have to come out of the back of a European grimoire. It can come from yourself, with what you have around you and come from the spirits that may guide your hand through the process.

Is somebody you know in dire need of protection, and they also happen to also practice black smithery? Easy! Take the water in the forge that was used to quench the hot iron and pour it over the front and back door of the threshold to cool down even the hottest of bewitchments or intense malevolence that could be sent their way. With the imbuing of iron and its protective virtues into that water, it serves as a strong protective agent. Do they not practice black smithery? Take some holy water from a church or well water, heat up some iron, and speak your intentions of protection and then quench the hot iron with the water aspersing it onto the doorways of the threshold. There is always a way around things that suits to what we have around us. Needing a bit more money? Gather clover, St John's wort, and marigolds for prosperity, along with rosemary for protecting your finances. Get hold of a cash book from the bank and inscribe a psalm within it or a bible passage that speaks of money and secrete it into the charm. don't want to get religious? Clearly write your petition to what you desire financially on the cheque, whilst charging it with your intention over the gathered plants and tie it together along with your will using a red string for power and hang it in the centre of the household. Years ago, the centre of the home used to be the hearth but sadly many people do not have hearths these days, so the kitchen is the hearth of the home and feeds people so that's the best thing. Do you feel you're needing a little bit more luck? Find an empty snail shell and input into it herbs associated with luck such as heather or a four leafed clover and perhaps a petition of your intent, sealing it with wax and carry it with you to help bring this about. Is somebody from your workplace proving to be difficult? Take a dishcloth from your place of working, and fashion a doll out of it. include the person in questions name along with some of their personal effects, baptising the doll in their name whilst inputting it into a clear jar with a screw on lid. Then each day for seven days, go and visit a river. Speak to the spirits of the river, tell them your plans to gain influence and control over the colleagues meddling ways and make sure each time you gather some water, leave an offering for them. Take the water home and each day speak your intentions into the water as if speaking to the person. Spit on it and top it up each day so that the doll absorbs the water and so absorbs your influences. Is it not working? Well, put a bit more pressure and start to fill the whole jar with the water bit by bit, making sure they are overflowed with your power and unable to move away from the enchantment, once they submit, take it out.

    The folk magic you practice can be more powerful for you than older spells. Just because a spell is old, doesn't mean that will automatically make it viably effective for you. I have worked old conjurations and spells that for me haven't worked at all and I have worked some that have worked very well for me. It's about finding what works for you, for instance over the years of practicing I have a healing spell that never fails me. It's not an ancient spell, it's not a spell found in a grimoire from the seventeenth century, its completely new. Whenever I need to heal somebody, I know that I can go to that spell, and it will be successful for me. Don't be afraid to start your own traditions in spells and charms.

It's about making sure what you're practicing is working for you and others you're intending your will for. Its ok to base new spells too off old ones, for instance the famous charm by Scottish accused witch Isobel Gowdie, gave a charm that went as such:

"He is laying there sick and sore,

Let him lie there seven days more!"

We could change that to the persons full name, and if we're away from the ill person in bed. This is a perfect charm to make sure that they are bound whilst we are unable to be present. A chant of this could be worked up over and over focusing the intent upon that person, visualising your will taking place. As mentioned earlier in this book, if we don't adopt British folk magic to the now how can it as a tradition possibly survive?

Devices Of the Spirit world: Contacting the invisible

Throughout the history of British folk magic, be its more beneficial counterpart the cunning folk or within the realms of the more sinistral idea of the witch, spirits have always played a part within folk magic. Their uses are varied throughout different historical accounts, but they have always been employed to fuel the magic or to even to grant specific desires in which the magician favoured. One of the most mentioned spirits in terms of the practice of popular magic, seems to arise form the idea of the familiar spirit. This is what's known as a fetch or spirit in which has a close companionship with the practitioner. There seems to be this element of: you scratch my back, il scratch your back. After all a relationship with anybody, must be reciprocal and must benefit the persons concerned.

To put this into context, if I was to walk over to a stranger on the street and ask them for £20 the likelihood, I'm going to get that money from the stranger is very small and second to none. However, if I walked up to a close friend and told them how I was in trouble and needed that money and id buy them a pint in the future, the chances of me getting that increase. Now don't get me wrong, you don't set up relationships with spirits or anybody with that matter to score £20! My point is, it must work both ways and you're much better working with spirits with whom you are familiar with. Hence the term familiar spirit. An aspect when working with spirits which shows up in witch trials and accounts often is the idea of a pact: You scratch my back, il scratch yours. In other words, if you do this for me then il do the following thing for you. Making pacts with spirits tend to be very effective at causing what it is you desire to come to fruition. When making and establishing a pact with a spirit, always remember that it is binding and sealing. So, you must keep extremely mindful of what promises you've made. As breaking that promise can not only result in devastating effects to what it is you're conjuring, but it also will become inevitable of fracturing the relationship and companionship with that spirit.

What exactly do familiar spirits look like? And what are the types of spirits that can be classed as a familiar? In truth, all, and many. Like I've mentioned before, if it's a particular spirit you have a close bond with and a relationship where you're familiar with then that's the part they become a familiar spirit. A familiar spirit can technically be an ancestor in which you've had a close bond with and somebody who lends their help during any workings you do. It could be a faery folk that's taken a liking to you, even an animal spirit with whom you had a closeness with when they were alive, an angelic intelligence that has always made itself known to you, or an infernal spirit that tends to hang around you. The point is, familiar spirits come in all shapes and sizes and can be different types of spirits. If we pay attention to history, we only need to look at witch trials and cunning folk practices to see the myriad of familiar spirits. Tom Reid mentioned earlier was the spirit of a war soldier who passed away who become the familiar spirit and helper of Bessie Dunlop. Joan Upney's two spirits in the case of the Dagenham witches, one a mole and the other a toad.

A ritual of communication

It was always said that Cecil Williamson claimed he would speak with his 'shadow' an hour a night to keep up the companionship and bond between himself and familiar spirit. Regarding this working, Cecil's evening ritual is something that has become a huge inspiration behind the following ritual. Before we begin, I want you all to know this ritual isn't the same as any of the others found in this book. What is interesting is that a lot of the time, we tend to find that in modern witchcraft traditions there has been an uprise and surge in the magical taking of effect via the internal map of the witch/magician. Many of these practices involve what is known as shadow work, emotional healing and mindfulness techniques. Such rituals or 'spells' are fast on the uprise in terms of popularity which mostly can leave a bitter taste in the folk magician's mouth. Once again let me be perfectly clear, most of the folk magic I practice tends to revolve around affecting the world around me rather than my own internal emotions or feelings. Personally, I wouldn't class these acts of affecting the mind and emotions as 'spells' in a sense. However, I absolutely would not criticise any witch or magician for utilising these practices, as I do feel these modern practices radiate the need for more mindfulness in the fast and sometimes unforgiving contemporary world.

This ritual is what's known as a ritual of communication, and it is something that just came to me in a time that I genuinely really needed it most. I am glad it did come at that time, as it pulled me through times that were quite frankly traumatic, and I fully believe that it saved my life. This isn't a spell or a charm at all and isn't designed to necessarily bring results to a physical degree but can leave change after has been completed if requested by the practitioner, it will generally create effects of synchronicity and what's known as omens to help guide the witch experiencing trauma (that being said it has brought results when asked for change.) All the ritual requires from you really is for you to speak from your heart. To open yourself up and to be naked almost in front of the spirits, helping connect you even more to the spirits in which whom you work with and have a relationship with. Truth is something that most humans stray away from in terms of how they truly feel through fear of hurting others around them or through fear of sounding selfish or stupid but if we feel like this it can make us feel trapped and depressed. Being human, there are things that we must let out otherwise we can become confused, depressed or it can even have an ugly effect on others around us. To do this ritual, you can start off by giving an offering. This can be as simple as a glass of water or coffee, but you can go as far out in terms of how much you give as you want. Secondly comfort. Make sure you're fully comfortable and in a place where you're able to express how you feel without prying eyes or prying ears snooping in on your conversation with the spirits.

To begin, light candles in the name of the spirits in which you work with, or you can always just use an invocation from your heart and call a myriad of different spirits you work with. It's entirely your choice, for instance the ancestors could be called as such:

"Ancestors here my prayers, blood of my blood, bone of my bone, spirit of my spirit, those whose faces reside in mine, those whose hearts beat within mine, ancestral spirits hear my call, hear my cries and be present in this time and in my truthfulness."

in the case of the familiar spirits that you work with:

"Spirits familiar unto me (name of familiar) by my will I call you and ask you to be present my friend, my companion, my confidant, hear my call hear my cries, and be present in this time and in my truthfulness."

After this has been done, make sure the offering has been given along with an explanation that you're needing to be truthful and honest with them about a situation. State that you're not only giving your offerings but you're giving your honesty as a sacrifice. Such an offering of complete and utter truthfulness really is something in my experience spirits appreciate. Let them know you're not wanting any change (you may however want change in which case state that you do) but rather you're needing a friend to listen to you. Then take a deep breath and from that moment, explain your full situation but don't skimp on the emotions, POUR YOUR HEART OUT. If you need to cry then cry. If you need to moan then moan, if you speak from your heart and create an avenue of truthfulness that you feel you cannot stop then you're completely on the right track. Once you've had your moment, then thank the spirits, extinguish the candles and the rite has ended. This rite came to me during the first lockdown. At the time with lockdown aside, I was going through some major changes in my life that were quite frankly heart-breaking and traumatising which landed me in a very troubling place to say the least. I fully know in my heart of hearts, this rite saved me. If this rite has that effect on just one person, then il be happy not just as a witch, but as a human being.

The Faery Faith

The Faery, Good Folk, Sidhe, little people, Pherishers, Pharisees, fair folk, they go by many names depending on the regions of Britain and Ireland, and yet their legacy really has a hold on the lands throughout the UK and Ireland. Throughout the ages, Britain has been flooded with tales and stories of the Good Folk and their ways. Such as the story of Thomas the rhymer, a young man taken by the Queen of Elphame who resides in the fairy otherworld for seven years and comes back with the ability of prophesy as well as having the inability to tell a lie again, hence the name he became known as afterwards; true Thomas. Another interesting story involves the faerie oak of Corriewater, involving the good people coming out from the hills to celebrate at a thousand-year-old oak that the queen of Elphame had planted. The reason for the celebration, is that the Queen of Elphen had sealed a deal with a kiss from a man known as Elph Irving who would give her his service for seven years. These stories and pieces of lore, emulate our ancestors' ways of thinking. The very idea that the land had spirits that resided within it, that had a separate world from ours with separate morals, beliefs, and ways and could influence others In a profound myriad of ways. Their otherworldly influences on people varied greatly from the beneficial such as bestowing gifts of music, the gift of prophesy, song, the giving of charms to help attain any needs, healing, protecting children and cattle to the more sinister examples. Such as child abduction and swapping fairy changelings unbeknown to the people around them, making people or cattle ill, stealing items, making people fairy-led which involves the poor unsuspecting individuals becoming lost forcing them to continuously walk in circles unbeknown of where they are, or in some even more sinister stories involving forcing people to drag dead bodies through the woods on their back until the crack of dawn. These situations and stories vary due to the nature of the Good Folk themselves. Another aspect was the idea that the fae folk had different courts they would originate from and inhabit.

    Typically, this was split into two groups Seelie and Unseelie. The Seelie were seen as those that would generally be fonder of humans and help humans and their ways. Whereas the Unseelie were seen as a more 'darker' court of fairy which would tend to be more averse to humans and would be more in favour typically doing harm than good. However, this wasn't so clear cut much in the ways of spirits. Seelie could sometimes punish and harm humans, and Unseelie could also favour some humans. It's just that typically this is what reputation these courts were known for. There is also talk of the other world of the Good Folk which through the ages has gone by many names ascribed to various places around Britain such as: Elphame, Annwyn, ect. The fae folk and their ways as mentioned are varied. One of the many similarities that link different faery courts and tribes together, is that their world is the idea their ways are completely different from ours. Another similarity is that when it comes to them (such is my experience with most spirits) a promise is a promise. It is binding and sealed, so what you've said around them can be the contract. So being very cautious and mindful about what you say and do is a good base to practicing the fairy faith. They absolutely love a loophole, like a clause in a contract.

  Cunning folk, witches and Fae have always had an interesting relationship with each other. Such as Bessie Dunlop who claimed that the queen of fairies had sent her familiar spirit Tom Reid and instructed him to wait upon her. Andro man again had a similar connection concerning his familiar spirit who he described as in the 'likeness of a fair angel and clad in white clothes' but had also pointed out that his angelic familiar swears to the 'Queen of Elphen' drawing similarities with the familiar of Bessie Dunlop.

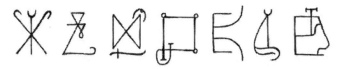

Sigil of the seven fairy sisters, taken from the grimoire of Arthur gauntlet.

How to work with the Good Folk

A WORD OF WARNING. When you're working with the Fae, be very careful what you say and how you say it. The faery folk LOVE loopholes and if there is the tiniest of loopholes in it, they'll jump. You must make sure you cover everything you talk about as if there is any way they are able to trick you, then by God, they'll do it. That's no to say they cannot be trusted, some of them can. However, their world is different to ours and a completely different way of doing things to the mundane human. I'm going to give an example here as to why:

A while back, a work colleague and a friend of mine had her wisdom tooth growing through and it was giving her horrific pain. With myself having conjured for her in the past, she asked me to do something. So, one evening a good friend of mine Jonathan Pheonix-Archer and myself, met up at a regular working site we both practiced in at the time. We stood between a two split tree and worked the charm over it, asking for the Good Folk to bless it with their influence and take away my friend's pain with her wisdom tooth. I had a slip of paper with her full name written onto it and via the use of transference, took an animal's tooth and rolled it into this piece of paper sealing it with red thread for strength as a small charm for my friend to carry. The next day after giving her the charm, she was still in pain and so I was sceptical being honest that our conjurations hadn't worked and taken effect. A couple of days later, it had stopped for her, and I realised that I had started to feel pain on the same side she had it. Low and behold my wisdom tooth had started growing through and hers had stopped! I couldn't eat on one side; I couldn't even talk properly. The inside of my cheek had been absolutely ripped to bits and I knew that something had not gone right. Returning to the site where we practice regularly, I spoke out loud to the good folk, and said: "Good folk, as happy as I am Maria is out of pain, I must ask why have I now got this wisdom tooth pain. I thought it had transferred into the tooth." My reply? "But it did of course transfer into the tooth! You said let it be transferred into the tooth. You didn't say WHAT tooth, now where's that offering you promised?" That right there, is a classic example of how they can find these loopholes.

    This doesn't mean the Fae are unfit to work with and will try to screw you over at any chance they get it, the Good folk have taught me things such as charms or spells for a dire need at that specific time, that have had great effect. They've also taught me things about myself which made a lot of sense and added things up for me, that however is between myself and the good folk. However, what I will say is that because there are so many of them from different courts or tribes, then that's when it can get varied. There are fae that absolutely hate humans and everything they stand for. Then there are those that will help lost children in woodlands like the Scottish Ghillie Dhu but may dislike humans who threaten the forest and then there are those that will have no qualms of dragging Children into a shallow watery grave such as Jenny Green teeth. Much in the way of people they're neutral but they have very different morals and ways than we do. Secondly, be kind and respectful, have we learnt nothing from the old fairy tales? What happens to the person who disrespects the beggar or shows a level of contempt for their fellow humans or any other living beings?? They end up paying a harsh price.

You never know who or what that beggar on the streets could be. Even if the beggar is a human just in a general perspective it pays to not be a dick! Another point that I would personally say from working with them, is that unless it's a helpful fae like a Brownie or a fae that is helping bring money and luck into somewhere, do NOT work with the fae in your house.

That is just something I have found from personal experience; things can get very weird for me if ive worked with them in the house. Electrics blow, things go bump in the night and ive had it that when ive been trying to sleep and ive felt their presence around me. Imagine feeling a hundred tiny eyes upon you from the darkness and you're trying to shut off? Doesn't happen and gets creepy fast. In the flats and houses ive stayed in, I have sometimes felt ancestral presences, absolutely fine. Familiar spirits that may even be fae themselves? Again, absolutely fine, their the spirits that protect and help you. The fae as a whole in my house? Absolutely not. In my opinion, I feel like the fae should be approached outside and worked with outside and given offerings outside too.

To start off with, venture to a Whitethorn tree (Hawthorn) which is a tree of the Fairy folk. Many people in Ireland will not cut them down as to do this is said to bring insult to the fairy folk and in result, is said to bring bad luck along with their wrath. This idea of the hawthorn being a fairy tree was also a prominent belief in England too, but sadly most people are unaware of this and deem it as silly superstition. There is also an instruction for gaining the aid of the otherworld through historical accounts and lore; Hawthorn does not have to be used, failing these other places that are associated with the Good Folk can be used such as: Burial mounds, stone circles, two split trees (also known as wishing trees.) Iron age forts, trees that have holes in the bottom of them acting as small doorways to Elphame also known as Pherisher trees in East Anglia or dolmens doors in the Midlands. Once at your sacred space to the wee folk, draw on the ground the seal of the seven faery sisters taken from the grimoire of Arthur gauntlet, the original ritual involving the seal is much different from my following ritual given. It's just utilising older practices alongside modern times. The foods you can use as offerings to the wee ones are cream, whole milk, butter, bread (especially homemade bread), things made by human hands are also favoured by them such as small gifts made for them such as small figures, coins, alcohol, honey, however generally as a curtesy to them, and to avoid their wrath there are certain guidelines you go by. The first rule is to be polite! Speak clearly and precisely making sure there aren't any loopholes as mentioned earlier. The actual ritual itself is simplistic. In short, it's basically venture to a hawthorn tree and sit by it for some time. Take your time and eventually you should start to feel a presence around you. If you sit under their tree long enough, they will notice. Once you've felt this immediate 'shift' in the atmosphere then start to talk to them. Introduce yourself to them and let them know who you are as a person, and what your intentions of going to see them are. After this has been done, then leave the offering under the tree and make them aware you've left offerings for them. Walk away and don't look back. This may take a couple of times, but eventually you will get yourself to a point where you'll notice them and see omens around you. Like building up any relationship these things take time. After a while has passed and you've done this as a regular thing weekly, for some time. You can then begin to ask them for their help and assistance in your workings. Once again, just be careful of what you say.

Isle of Mann charm against the faeries in the house

"Peace of God and Peace of man, Peace of God on columb-killey On each window and each door, On every hole admitting moonlight On the four corners of the house On the place of my rest And peace of God on myself."

-Folklore of isle of man

Graven Offerings: Working with the Dead

When the idea of working with the dead and magic are involved, it can often conjure up vivid images of  romanticism such as the famous artwork of the two famed magicians John Dee and Edward Kelly (left) summoning up a spirit in a dark cemetery. It has even become incorporated into elements of pop culture concerning witchcraft, such as the film sleepy hallow, where the witch holds the horseman's head, therefore holding power over him. Ceremonial magic, pop culture and practitioners aside, when it comes to folk magic historically working with the dead, there isn't as much information out there in terms of how to work with the dead than there is as opposed to say familiar spirits from witch trials and accounts. There are examples of course once again if we take our minds to Bessie Dunlop and Thom Reid. Despite Tom having access to Elphame and the world of wee folk, he wasn't himself a faery folk. He was a dead soldier, who had passed away in battle.

There is however when it comes to folklore, information on working with the dead and the ancestors. For example, in Cornwall it was customary to serve a table of people bread and cheese, whilst leaving the same dish on the windowsill with a light for the dead. In Irish and Scottish lore, there lies the famed dumb supper. The preparation of creating a meal for yourself and a meal for the dead that is to be eaten in complete and utter silence. The dead are served firstly, with everything taking place backwards, then the meal is to be eaten alongside with the dead. Lore can be applied when it comes to our own practice in conjunction when working with the dead. This is something that can not only bridge a gap between folk magic and contemporary practice, but also amplify our own spiritual practices. Another aspect that we tend to also forget is that when it comes to popish charms and conjurations working with the dead, the employment of saints does technically equate to working and veneration with the dead. In the eyes of the church and from conversations I've had with a Catholic priest, a saint is technically somebody who has passed away and gone to heaven. Of course, attached to saints comes the reputation of miracles and their workings. This can sometimes tend to cloud the very obvious fact stated in the latter. Remember, just because they have a halo doesn't mean they don't have a link to the spirit world. In terms of charming, another aspect is that there are some conjurations that employ the dead such as:

"Here come I to cure a burnt sore, if the dead knew what the living endure the burnt sore would burn no more."

There are also spells and charms that incorporate the use of the physical dead and their relics, such as the cure for a headache when a hang man's rope was employed to kill off headaches and other pains in the body. Another example being the famed hand of glory, which was said to be the hand of a hangman which would cause those sleeping to stay in an extremely deep sleep. There are more examples and although there isn't admittedly as many aspects of working with the dead within British folk magic as there is working with familiar spirit's, that doesn't mean we need to chuck the baby out with the bath water.

Working with your ancestors is an empowering and beautiful experience, that brings with it a lot of reward and fulfilment. By venerating and elevating your ancestors, you not only build powerful allies of protection, love, and support for your spell work, but for your personal life. You become closer with knowing yourself and who you are as a person. I once asked somebody close to me, about a large undertaking they were about to undergo in their life. The question I asked was: "aren't you scared?" Their reply: "Why should I be scared; I hold within my face, every face of every ancestor who's ever walked before me. They stand behind me." Such a statement resonated with me in a deep, personal, huge, and beautiful way and I think about this statement every time I undergo something big in my life. It is important to know that when working with the dead there are many ways this can be done. The first and foremost when working with the ancestral dead, is to set up a place of power for them or an altar. This isn't something that's historically evident within cunning folk practice, but it is found in other cultures as a way to honour and cherish the ancestral dead. Setting up an altar or a place of power for them is easy, have a clean table and onto this area, input things sacred to your ancestors. Typically, this could be your favourite pictures of them, funeral programs, perhaps beautiful items they've left to you after they've passed? Memorial candles? The list goes on and on when it comes to this. The altar can be decorated with so many different items that feel relevant to your own practice. After this has been done, sit and talk to them. Call them up in different ways. In the ritual of communication, I have included a conjuration that I speak when working with the ancestral dead:

"Ancestors hear my prayers, blood of my blood, bone of my bone, spirit of my spirit, those whose faces reside in mine, those whose hearts beat within mine, ancestral spirits hear my call, hear my cries and be present in this time and in my truthfulness."

     In truth working with the ancestors is one of the easiest things to do, as it's a given. You are literally the by-product of all your ancestors. Calling them when you already have that link established is a good call. Give regular offerings to them and feed them regularly, light candles in their name. A good thing to do when first working with them is to not ask for anything straight away, just feed them up. Elevate them for at least a couple of months, and keep giving them offerings. Regular talking to the space also helps, especially in the morning. There's nothing wrong with saying good morning to the ancestors before rushing out for work, it establishes that link and keeps the connection you have to the ancestors regular. It shows you still give your time. Keep in mind that birthdays and anniversaries can be dates that are that ancestor's feast day. Perhaps cooking them their favourite meals? Perhaps they had a favourite bunch of flowers they used to like? When working with the ancestors, even something so simple of how they made their brews can help show thoughtfulness and show that element of care. There are so many ways in order to work with the ancestral dead, and quite honestly if I was to list all the ways we would have another book on our hands.

 Other aspects of working with the dead is the unknown dead. These are spirits we aren't familiar with and who aren't ancestral. This can be tricky and sometimes dangerous. A word of warning, please be very careful when employing the unknown dead, as the wrong etiquette and clumsy attitudes can result in unwanted results. When working with the unknown dead, you have to bare in mind that like working with the ancestors this can be done in a myriad of ways. In fact, one of the charms included in this book involves working with the unknown dead. Once again, talking about this in more depth could result in a whole other book! So, when working with the unknown dead, wear some form of physical protection, such as rowan berry necklaces or a hag stone that will protect you against spiritual parasites. Like the fae, and really with anything in life, be polite and

63

always be wary of any promises made towards the unknown dead. Think before you speak tends to apply here. Necromancy with the unknown dead can be a dangerous path if the wrong intent is given or if unrealistic pacts are given. So, please for the love of God be cautious here.

Fetch of Fauna

From the natural world, another aspect of the familiar spirit is the working relationship of animal spirits. When  we speak of familiar spirits and the animal kingdom, people often have this idea that the familiar spirit is a pet. That's not the case and mostly rare in some cases, a familiar spirit is a spirit. It is mostly not a physical animal. They can be pets that you've had a relationship with, that you felt had a link to your practice and craft. So in the case of that pet passing away, they can be worked with as a familiar spirit. If of course, they want to. Another side to the animal kingdom, can be the fact that when walking in natural places such as woodlands or forests, we can sometimes stumble across the skulls or bodies of animals. This is something that can be gifted to us from the spirits of the land themselves, especially if we ask for a familiar spirit from spirits such as the folkloric devil but il go into that in due time. The skull in many past cultures such as Celtic cultures, was seen as the seat of the soul. When working with animal spirits you've not had a relationship with prior to its passing, its important to actually speak to that spirit.

The following ritual structure I got from Sarah Ann Lawless, who once shared it on her excellent previous blog she used to write, known as the witch of forest grove. Most of the content on the following working is heavily Influenced by her latter writings. Another point I may add here, is that the following rite is taken and heavily influenced from traditional witchcraft and so I want to make the statement I am not in any way shape or form pretending that it is the magic of the cunningfolk. Such a statement would be obscene and ridiculous, but seeing as we're speaking on familiar spirits and modern traditional witchcraft is based off older examples of folk magic, I wanted to include this. This ritual is one I have performed myself that has had incredible results. I think it only fair that by talking on familiar spirit's, that I'm able to give an actual rite or working that can achieve such a thing and gain spiritual companionship that will add to your workings and benefit your own practice.

On the night of the full moon, firstly talk to the skull of the animal and ask it if you can work with it as a spirit. This factor is important, as I've had bad mishaps in the past where this hasn't happened and its had stupid results due to me making a silly mistake. Like most undergoings with spirits, always ask permission. As enslaving a spirit and forcing it to do something against its will, isn't going to score you friendship points. After this has been done, start to then clean the skull up. Hold a cleansing ritual for the animal, washing away any past hurt or trauma so it doesn't carry into your practice ensuring trust between yourself and the creature is gained. Always remember, it's a two-way street. It has to work for them as it does for you. Make a wash out of holy water, silver and vervain. Using this concoction, wash away any pain and upset the creature has experienced in their lifetime. Whilst this is being done, speak sweet words of encouragement to the animal of love and apologise if the animal has suffered greatly at the hands of any fellow humans. Really put care and consideration into this act, let your true self be seen by the spirit as opening up to the animal will help gain understanding of you from the animals perspective. Next is time for fumigation, take any cleansing herbs such as pine, cedar, or juniper berries and fumigate the skull. Take a black shroud and cover the skull leaving it alone in an undisturbed place, for a whole lunar period from the full moon until the dark moon. A month later, when the dark moon arises, take the animals skull in the shroud still ensuring it remains completely covered until the ritual of reddening the bones occurs. Venture to a lonely place in the nighttime on your own, marking out a circle on the ground for your operations. In the centre of this circle, dig a shallow pit large enough to hold the skull in and three firelighters forming a triangle around the freshly dug pit. You can have 3 tealight candles but realistically outside, tealight candles do not stay lit and the point of this is by adding fire we add fuel and lifeforce to the skull and working. A good idea, is that the firelighters should be eco-friendly as normal everyday firelighters aren't beneficial at all to the environment and the wildlife. Especially when working with an animal (especially one that may have suffered at the hands of humans) we need to be mindful of the benefit the actual working will leave for the other lifeforms behind. Within this triangle, ensure that you have a vessel of tree resin burning as an offering to the spirit of who you're working for. Normally I would recommend dragons blood, as its deep red colour represents blood. However, due to over harvesting, dragons' blood is unfortunately becoming extinct. Other resins from trees such as cherry or plum, form a deep red colour and so can be burnt in substitute and act as a more sustainable choice.

Call on the folkloric devil also known as the Lord of beasts, asking him to lend his power and raise up the animal of the skull so that it can become your ally and familiar spirit that will help you within your arte. The following invocation to him can be worked:

"I call out to you, aulde Harry, aulde Scratch, aulde goat footed Devil of the crossroads and Lord of beasts I call out to you. Hear my call and come this night now to receive my supplications and offerings granting my request."

Once this is done, explain the above to him that you're wanting him to call back the spirit of the skull you're working with. In exchange for his power lended to the rite, pour a good offering such as whiskey or drink as a libation. Take the skull in the funeral shroud, opening it up and placing it within the pit. Use this time to whisper into the ear of the skull your intentions again and that you're wanting to work with it as a familiar spirit and why it is here this night. Remember, speak from your heart and be authentic.

Take red powdered red ochre, and recite the following as you redden the skull over and over again until the skull is covered with ochre:

*"White is the colour of bone and Ash,
We feed the dead we bathe and fast,
Black is the colour of womb and tomb,*

67

*We dance with the dead on the dark of the moon,
Red is the colour of blood and death,
We rub the bones To give them breath."*

    Once the skull has been completely reddened, start to pace around widdershins envisioning and visualising the skull glowing red with life. Build up this pacing motion for some time, reciting the chant above and keeping envisioned the glowing red skull pulsing with lifeforce. Now comes the time to make a deal with that spirit, to make a pact. Speak clearly and ask them to let you know if the deal is acceptable to them, and if you've done this correctly, you'll know. You'll feel it deep in your core and soul that you've made the right deal for them. It's not always a given, sometimes you'll need to speak a couple of deals but remember to always keep them and to follow through on your promise. Once this pact is made and agreed, spill some blood for the spirit as a symbol of that pact and a link between yourself and your new spiritual companion via use of a medicinal lancet. Pouring some of that blood onto the spirits vessel. Afterwards, offer the spirit some good drink and some food in the form of a libation. Food can be anything from bread to a homemade cake but normally something that crumbles and isn't harmful to the outdoor wildlife.

    Once this is done, pack up taking the skull with you, get home, pour yourself a hot chocolate, and unwind. It is at this point after the ritual, the skull itself becomes the familiars spirit house. Clean it, talk to it weekly, and feed it regular offerings, keeping and maintaining its spirit house so that it is well looked after and well-fed. After all, a well-fed spirit is a happy spirit!

The Fetch or Nocturnal Servitor

Another aspect of spirit work and familiar spirit's in general, is what's known as the Nocturnal servitor. These spirit's aren't necessarily a familiar that presents itself to the practitioner offering some pact or deal. Instead, they're created by the practitioner themselves, and created for a sole purpose and reason. These types of spirit's can be found within certain practices of ceremonial magic, but aren't limited only to high magic. Within folk magic, they play their own part and are extremely effective and efficient at achieving an end goal or desire. The spirit is created from the energy of the magician, inputting into the fetch their will of what they are wanting to achieve and accomplish. From this point, it is given a spirit house that it inhabits which we will go into more detail in the next section.

    Typically the spirit is given a time limit and a deadline and is told by that particular date when their job has been complete, that they will cease to exist. It is very important that they are destroyed once the key purpose for their existence has been achieved. These spirit's left with nothing to do and left to their own devices can become very troublesome, draining life-force from the magician, creating problems in the practitioners lives, and they can actually become more of a spiritual parasite if left to their own devices after their sole purpose is achieved. There are some cases when folks have made a fetch and not destroyed it. However, these tend to be for a specific cause that may take some time and typically, its always best when creating a fetch to give them a short life span.

Creating a spirit is relatively easy to do and I'm going to go more into this the way I was taught. To begin with, take both hands and cup them together envisioning energy going from yourself into your hands, whilst forming a ball of light in your mind's eye. Keep this visualisation going and start to input more energy into this ball of light gradually visualising it growing bigger and bigger. Start to chant the name that youre calling your spirit. It is incredibly important at this point to keep the name of this spirit completely secret. As knowing the name of a spirit, is to have power over it and it can be extremely dangerous giving somebody else that name, thereby giving them authority over that spirit. Which in the wrong hands could prove fatal. Disclaimers aside, start to chant the name of the spirit over and over again. Repeating the name of the fetch, and pumping energy from yourself into this ball of white light. With this being done, and still repeating the name of the spirit then start to form shape to the fetch. Perhaps he is used to cut away a negative person from your life? Maybe he'll have scissors for hands? Maybe she is a protective spirit? Perhaps she'll have a large shield and sword? Make the spirit appear to the qualities you're wanting to draw. Once the shaping of this spirit is done and you're fully visualising this spirit in front of you, then give the statement of intention to the spirit. Remember be completely crystal clear as of the following: what you're naming it, who created it, what it's sole purpose is, when it will complete the task, and lastly when it will be destroyed. The following is a statement of intention I'm giving as an example so that you're able to tailor your specific needs to it:

"Your name is Pyewackett, you are created by myself and myself alone. You're created for the sole purpose and the purpose alone of ensuring that I am fully protected against all harm whilst I travel in the country of India until the 30th of April 2022 and once your purpose is complete, on that date you will be completely destroyed and you will cease to exist and be no more."

Once the spirit is created, it is important to feed the spirit. The simplest way to do that is a couple of drops of your blood every week. By doing this, you're imbuing it not only with your physical essence but you're wanting something to work that much, you're willing to draw blood for it. Blood is life-force and by giving the spirit this, amplifies its power and allows it to become a living and breathing embodiment in order to carry your will.

Once the fetch has completed their task, they are then to be destroyed. I have to stress again this is the most **IMPORTANT** part of creating a spiritual servitor, as mentioned above. When left to their own devices, they can become problematic. For destroying the servitor, you'll need a pair of scissors. Call the spirit to you by repeating its name, and start to see and envision your fetch appearing before you stating the following:

"Pyewackett you have completed your soul task of protecting me whilst I was travelling through India. You will now completely cease to exist. I now completely destroy you. You are no more"

Take the scissors and cut into the spirit, that's right. Cut. Start to cut up the spirit, over and over again into small pieces and see it starting to completely disperse. You can then take a broom and sweep away the area to the directions of North, east, south and west and walk away without looking back. Any spirit houses that were made are to be dismantled and sprinkled with holy water to cleanse away the ties and influence of the previous fetch.

Of Spirit Houses and Fetishes

Once you have established an active relationship and agreed a pact with a particular familiar spirit, it is important for you to keep a spirit house. These houses can vary greatly and there have been so many different examples of them throughout different time periods in history. A spirit house is basically an object, or a number of items attached to one, that hold and house a spirit within their own free will. If you put this into thought, by working with a spirit and giving them a house or an item of power, they are free to inhabit, you're basically giving them a link to the physical world, as that item will be made and come from the earth. By doing this action, it allows the spirit to keep one foot in this world and one foot in the other. Thus, not only acting as a messenger but also giving them influence within the mundane.

These houses can range from very basic and simplistic such as a designated pot under the cupboard, to elaborate and beautifully crafted items such as sticks with twine attached and holed stones and shells similar to baby's cot mobiles, fascinating and occupying the spirit. A well-known and common trait in British folklore, is that spirits will feel compelled to count a number of objects. What's also incredibly useful is that the spirit houses holding different items to count aren't just set at familiar spirits, they can be used and placed into the threshold for troublesome spirits, keeping them busy enough to not cause any trouble, bumps in the night, or general disturbances in the house. So for instance, there have been spirit houses found that hold in them different items to help achieve this. Such as bottles filled with knotted string and cord, multiple amounts of seeds, different coloured stones, various pieces of sea glass that have been found, and even at times the popular cake decorations known as hundreds and thousands! These items of power or fetishes are in essence intact and physical spirit, once again representing the physical link of that working spirit in the mundane. So, always ensure that these houses are cleaned and spoken to regularly, and above all well fed! Always give suitable offerings to familiar spirits, not only to give them strength, but to also ensure that working relationship keeps going and always well established.

When crafting a spirit house, always ask the spirit you're working with what kind of a spirit house they're wanting or desiring. You should from that point get a feeling or an image in your head of what you're wanting it to look like. Once again, let creativity guide you and use your imagination here. Crafting one isn't as difficult and as hard as you may think. Talk to the spirit beforehand, tell them that you're creating a spirit house designated only for them and ask them to guide you in its making so that they're happy with it. Allow yourself as you're making the fetish to go into a deep trance. Keep the particular spirit in your mind at all times here, asking for their influence once again on the house you're making. After the fetish has been created and crafted, it is now time to dedicate the vessel to your familiar spirit.

Take some white chalk, and draw a triangle onto the floor, along with three lit tealights in the corners of the triangle. Then into the centre, input your spirit house and speak aloud to the spirit you're addressing:

> *"Pyewackett, ive made this vessel for you as a way to show you my love and appreciation. I give you this spirit house and ask that you work for me as my familiar spirit and help me in my workings."*

This is an example, but the point of this is speak from your heart and be truthful about it! If you're going to start a working relationship with a spirit, then perhaps keeping things honest from the get go is a way to get onto a winner.

The Conjurations for the days of the week

Image taken from Francis Barretts the Magus

The powers of the planets and their influences over people, played an important part certain cunning folk practices. Many would consult the stars before making decisions or draw up people's astrological charts such as James cunning Murrell, in the remnants of one of his books showing an astrological chart for queen Victoria. The methods of astrology within cunning folk practices ranged once again in a myriad of ways from the simplistic to the elaborate from working with planetary squares as talismans to large arduous conjurations. One of the staples of the western magical tradition was Cornelious Agrippas *four books of occult philosophy,* in which they held in them planetary conjurations for the days of the week. These conjurations work with the angelic intelligences that each rule over a specific planet that governs specific influences the cunning person or magician would want to use. These conjurations then went on to be found in grimoires of cunning folk such as the grimoire of Arthur gauntlet. The acts of planetary conjurations were also featured within Francis Barrett's the magus, which was a book that had influenced the practices of cunning folk in the 1800s and through to the early 1900s. Despite the conjurations for the days of the week being typically used and worked within the realms of ceremonial magic, cunning folk such as cunning Murrell had copied pages from the magus in little manuscripts that were left of his books before they were reportedly burnt.

A Table shewing the names of the Angels governing the 7 days of the week, with their Sigils, Planets, Signs, &c.

Sunday	Monday	Tuesday	Wednesday	Thursday	Friday	Saturday
Michael	Gabriel	Camael	Raphael	Sachiel	Aniel	Caffiel
☉	☽	♂ ♈ ♏	☿ ♊ ♍	♃ ♐ ♓	♀ ♉ ♎	♄ ♑ ♒
name of the 1.st Heaven	name of the 2.nd Heaven	name of the 3.rd Heaven	name of the 4.th Heaven	name of the 5.th Heaven	name of the 6.th Heaven	ye 7 Angels ruling above the 7 Heavens
Machen.	Shamain.	Machon.	Raquie.	Zebul.	Sagun.	

It was not uncommon for cunning folk to utilise ceremonial magic and blend it into rural folk magic, forming a basis of folk-ceremonial magic which are demonstrated in these grimoires and manuscripts mentioned. With the spirit of folk ceremonial adaptions from cunning folk and their practices, I am going to go into a way that I simplistically work with the conjurations for the days of the week. Initially, these conjurations were done within a circle, involving a consecration and exorcism as well as putting a vesture on and orations to God. For the sake of origin and referencing I have included part of the conjuration for a circle, however there are a lot more steps involved prior to the operation and within this rite in general. Please bare this in mind when it comes to this working. If I was to go into everything that is involved in these planetary conjurations, then I feel we would miss more folk centred magic in which will then defeat the point of this book. If anybody reading this is interested in the full ceremonial operations of these planetary intelligences, then I urge you to investigate the magus by Francis Barrett or investigate the full ritual in Agrippa's four books of occult philosophy. The circle itself if made three times, being nine foot in diameter and on top of this will always change on inscription depending on which planetary intelligence you're conjuring and calling as well as planetary hours involved. The aforesaid being mentioned, here is the conjuration for the circle:

"in the name of the holy, blessed, and glorious trinity proceed we to our work in these mysteries to accomplish that which we desire; we therefore, in the names aforesaid, consecrate this piece of ground for our defence, so that no spirit whatever shall be able to break these boundaries, neirther be able to cause injury nor

detriment to any of us here assembled; but that they may be compelled to stand before this circle, and to answer truly our demands, so far as it pleaseth him who liveth for evr and ever; and who says I am alpha and omega, the beginning and the end which is, and which was, and which is to come, the Almighty; I am first and the last, who am living and was dead, and behold I live for ever and ever; and I have the keys of death and hell. Bless O Lord I this creature of earth wherein we stand; confirm, O God! Thy strength in us, so that neither the adversary not any evil thing may cause us to fail, through the merits of Jesus Christ amen."

    The formula I have created is much more simplistic than this and is working with the aspect of folk magic rather than ceremonial. I also want to take this moment to thank a friend of mine John-David Kelly a fantastic and knowledgeable astrologer who taught me a way to work with the planets and their influences within his practice. It is from him that ive become inspired to input the daily conjurations into this book, as it has genuinely added to my practice. A simple outline for this folk-ceremonial rite, is to take some liquid chalk if indoors and inscribe the symbols of the celestial intelligence you're wishing to consult onto the floor. After this has been done, take a candle representing the colour of the angelic being you're wishing to have influence over you favour asked. If outdoors, the seals can still be inscribed into the earth with a stick. To start off with, making a basic incense blend of the resins and herbs that are associated with the corresponding planet you're working with is a good first step. This incense can be used to give as an offering to the angelic intelligences in exchange for what it is you're petitioning for. I am going to supply a range of incenses that correspond to the ruling planets, however, please be aware that some of these plants and herbs are poisonous and proper research of them should be done before burning them as incense:

The Sun: Marigolds, celandine, Frankincense, sunflower, red sanders, rosemary, chamomile, cedarwood.

The Moon: Lady's mantle, myrtle, bay, myrrh, poppies, iris, willow, juniper, mugwort, aloes.

Mars: pepper, cypress, nettles, tobacco, sweet basil, wormwood, hawthorn, hedge mustard, ginger, gorse, pepper.

Mercury: cinnamon, marjoram, lavender, liquorice, honeysuckle, fennel, fern, forget-me-not, heather, mastic.

Jupiter: agrimony, borage, hyssop, sage, houseleek, wood betony, dandelion, grapefruit, saffron.

Venus: Rose, geranium, violet, vervain, strawberry, cherry tree, devils' bit, pepperwort.

Saturn: Myrrh, musk, patchouli, Wolfs bane (aconite), sulphur, blackthorn, aspen, horsetail, sulphur.

These incenses I have made on the day of Wednesday the day of mercury as mercury is the planet of communication which will help to establish communication to the other planets, and they are compounded in the hours of the planet you wish to work with. Not to overcomplicate things though, but if you're wanting to also create your incenses a week prior to the day of the conjuration you're working with that's also fine. A good thing John-David told me, was a good time to work with the planetary intelligences is at sunrise on the day of the conjuration you wish to make. As at that moment, the planet starts its ruling influence on the day and in doing so is at its most potent. So, performing these conjurations at sunrise is a good way to connect to the planetary intelligences you're working with. Each ruling planets have their own seals, which can be drawn upon the floor in chalk the night before the working.

A conjuration for Sunday

Ruling angel: Michael (meaning who is like God or gift from God)

Influences: success, health and vitality, wealth, warmth.

"I conjure and confirm upon you, ye strong and holy angels of God, in the name of Adonai, eye, eye, eya, which is he who was, and is, and is to come, Eye, Abray; and in the name Saday, Cados, Cados, sitting on high upon the cherubin; and by the great name of God himself, strong and powerful, who is exalted above all the heavens; ye, Saraye, who created the world, the heavens, the earth, the fea, and all that in them is, in the first day, and sealed them with his holy name Phaa, and by the name of the angels who rule in the fourth heaven, and serve before the most mighty Salamia, an angel great and honourable, and by the name of his star, which is Sol, and by his sign, and by the immense name of the living God, and by all the names aforesaid, I conjure thee, Michael, O great angel! Who art chief ruler of this day; and by the name Adonai, the God of Israel, I conjure thee, O Michael! That thou labour for me, and fulfil all my petitions according to my will and desire in my cause and business."

A conjuration for Monday

Ruling angel: Gabriel (meaning God is my strength)

Influences: Divination, Dreams, intuition, psychic ability.

"I conjure and confirm upon you, ye strong and good angels, in the name Adonai, Adonai, Adonai, Adonai, Eye, Eye, Eye; Cados, Cados, Cados, Achim, Achim, Ja, Ja, strong Ja, who appeared in mount Sinai with the glorification of king Adonai, Sadai, Zebaoth, Anathay, Ya, Ya, Ya, Maranata, Abim, Jeia, who created the sea and all the lakes and waters, in the second day, which are above the heavens and in the earth, and sealed the sea in his high name, and gave it its bounds beyond which it cannot pass; and by the names of the Angels who rule the first legion, and who serve Orphaniel, a great, precious, and honourable angel, and by the name of his star which is Luna, and by all the names aforesaid, I conjure thee, Gabriel, who art chief ruler of Monday, the second day, that thou labour and fulfil

A Conjuration for Tuesday

Ruling angel: Samuel (meaning poison of God)

Influences: revenge, confrontation, soldier, iron

"I conjure and call upon you, ye strong and good angels, in the names of Ya, Ya, Ya He, He, He; Va, Hy, Hy, Ha, Ha, Ha, Va, Va, Va; An, An, An, Aia, Aia, Aia, El, Ay, Elibra, Elohim, Elohim; and by the names of the High God, who hath made the sea and dry land, and by his word hath made the earth, and produced trees, and hath set his seal upon the planets, with his precious,

honoured, revered and holy name; and by the name of the angels governing in the fifth house, who are subservient to the great angel Acimoy who is strong, powerful, and honoured, and by the name of his star which is Mars, I call upon thee Samuel, by the names above mentioned, thou great angel! Who presides over the day of Mars, and by the name Adonai, the living and true God, that you assist me in accomplishing my labours and fullfill

A Conjuration for Wednesday

Ruling angel: Raphael (meaning to heal/God healed)

Influences: communication, theft, trickery.

"I conjure and call upon you, ye strong and holy angels, good and powerful, in a strong name of fear and praise, Ja, Adonay, Elohim, Saday, Saday, Saday; Eie, Eie, Eie; Afamie, Afamie; and in the name of Adonay. The God of Israel, who hath made the two great lights, and distinguished day from night for the benefit of his creatures; and by the names of all the discerning angels, governing openly in the second house before the great angel, Tetra , strong and powerful; and by the name of his star which is Mercury; and by the name of his seal, which is that of a poweful and honoured God, and I call upon thee Raphael, and by the names above mentioned, thou great angel who presidest over the fourth day: and by the holy name which is written in the front of Aaron, createdthe most high priest, and by the names of all the angels who are constant in the grace of Christ, and by the name and place of Ammalium, that you assist me in my labours and &&"

A conjuration for Thursday

Angel: Sachiel (meaning the covering of God)

Influences: Jovialness, royalty, abundance, prosperity.

"I CONJURE and confirm upon you, ye strong and holy angels, by the names Cados, Cados, Cados, Eschereie, Eschereie, Eschereie, Hatim, Ya, strong founder of the worlds, Cantine, Jaym, Janic, Anic, Calbot, Sabbac, Berisay, Alnaym; and by the name Adonai, who created fishes and creeping things in the waters, and birds upon the face of the earth, flying towards heaven, in the fifth host before Pastor, a holy angel a great and powerful Prince and by the name of his star, which is Jupiter, and by the name of his seal, and by the name of Adonai, the great God, creator of all things and by the names of all the stars, and by their power and virtue, and by all the names aforesaid, I conjure thee, Sachiel, a great angel, who art chief ruler of Thursday, that for me thou labour for me"

A Conjuration for Friday

Angel: Haniel (meaning joy of God)

Influences: Love/friendships, beauty, riches, lust.

"I CONJURE and confirm upon you , ye strong and holy angels, by the names On, Hey, Heya, Ja, Je, Saday, Adonai, and in the name of Sadai, who created four footed beasts, and creeping things, and man, in the

sixth day, and gave to Adam power over all creatures; wherefore blessed be the name of the creator in his place; and by the name of the angels serving in the third host, before Dagiel, a great angel, and a strong and powerful prince, and by the name of his star which is Venus, and by his seal which is holy; and by the names of the aforesaid, I conjure upon thee, Anael, which art the chief ruler of this day, that thou labour for me."

A Conjuration for Saturday

Angel: Cassiel (meaning cover of God)

Influences: stillness, cursing, spirits, darkness.

"*I conjure and confirm upon you, Caphriel or cassiel, machator, and seraquiel, strong and powerful angels; and by the name Adonai, Adonai, Adonai, Eie, Eie, Eie; Acim, Acim, Acim; Cados, Cados, Cados; Ima, Ima, Ima; Salay, Ja, Sar, Lord and maker of the world, who rested on the seventh day; and by him who of his good pleasure gave the fame to be observed by the children of Israel throughout their generations, that they shouldkeep and sanctify the fame, to have thereby a good reward in the world to come; and by the names of his star which is Saturn; and by his holy seal, and by the aforesaid names spoken, I conjure upon thee, Caphriel, who art chief ruler of the seventh day, which is the sabbath, that for me thou labour.*"

Benedictions:
Healing and charming

To Transfer the Toothache

This spell is an older spell however, it has been adapted with other aspects of historical British folk magic and is a personal one from my own book I carry around when the need arises to practice. The reason I want to share this with you all in this instance, is of how it was utilised to what I had around me at the time. As mentioned, in terms of using what you have around you is an integral part of folk magic. A lot of cunning folks typically had to make use of what was around them. Particularly regarding the more rural/working class cunning folk, who couldn't afford to invest in a separate bowl for charming techniques such as hallowing waters or feeding Spirit/Fairy allies.

This charm was performed for a previous work colleague and good friend, who had been suffering quite a painful toothache at the time. A vessel was taken, with a small amount of water was poured in, I also made use of a

5 pence piece. The idea of 'silvering' the water which comes from a Scottish practice of hallowing objects particularly water, for use of magical purpose. A good friend of mine Ash William Mills, carries around with him a silver sixpence for the use of hallowing water in case the need ever arises. This practice is mentioned in different texts regarding curing bewitchment such as in rowan tree and red thread. Where a woman cures the evil eye borrowing a sixpence from a neighbour and working it into the charm to counteract the evil eye that had befallen the victim. One of the reasons that the six pence is used, is the fact they were also partly made from silver.

However, five pence pieces don't hold any silver within them at all. So, in this instance I had to make use of what was around me. I used something silver in colour drawing on the sympathetic element of it rather than its actual chemical element, which worked well enough. A moment is taken, and the silver object is whispered over asking for it to transfer the toothache into the water, asking this in the name of Saint Peter and Jesus as the charm itself incorporates the two together. The silver object is then crossed over the vessel three times. Encircling the cross in a clockwise motion each time and then it is dropped into the vessel. The practitioner places both hands over the vessel of hallowed water and mutters the following charm three times:

"As peter sat on a tomb stone, Up came Jesus and he alone, Oh Peter, Peter why do you ache? Oh, my Lord and Saviour it is the toothache, Rise up Peter and be healed and anyone that says this prayer three times by day and three times by night, shall never suffer from the pains of the toothache. "

at the end of the charm, It was stated very clearly: *"Let it be done, let it be done, let it be done."* The silver is then taken out of the water, which is then given to the client who takes the water and swills it around their mouth much in the same way as if it were mouthwash spitting the water back out into the vessel. The vessel of water is then poured onto a nearby tree, thus transferring the toothache pain into the tree from the patient. I want to add, this charm was not performed in an ancient woodland, by a sacred well or spring. This charm was performed in a shopping mall and worked very well! I poured the water onto a tree that was inside the shopping mall. Another thing I will add onto this in terms of instruction, is make sure the tree or plant you're transferring the pain to is real as sadly, a lot of public spaces have been making use of plastic plants as decoration rather than the real deal. To transfer the pain, the vessel that receives it must be living. Plants will also suffice, failing this a lawn of grass.

Family Wart Charm

As mentioned earlier, the following charm is a family charm given to me by my dad, told by his mum, who was then taught by her mum Sarah Ann Reeder. Its once again very simplistic and practical, as folk magic often is and involves the use of a piece of ham or bacon. The piece of ham is rubbed onto a wart and flushed down the toilet and the person performing this charm must not tell a single soul and forget about what they've done. My dad performed this with my sister on a troublesome skin tag and it disappeared and went away.

The Nightmare Stone

A holed stone threaded through, which was named: "a nightmare stone" which is in the Horniman museum, was used by a policeman named 'Hitch' and given to the museum in 1906. This stone was said to ward away any nightmares or any evil spirits that may be responsible nightmares. There also exists a charm in reginald scots discoverie of witchcraft, which calls for the influence of St George and a holed hag stone which is hung over the person bed to protect against nightmares and inccubus:

> "St George, St George, Our Ladys Knight,
> he walks by day, so does he by night,
> and when he had her found,
> he her beat, and he her bound
> until to him, her troth she plight,
> she would ot stir from him that night."

There is also a display in the west highland folk museum in Fort William, featuring the instructions from a Misses Macphee and Mrs Mackean in Helensburgh which is a Cure for a Nightmare:

> "Hang a stone over the affected persons bed which stone hath naturally such a hole in it as wherein a string may be put through it and so be hanged over the diseased or bewitched party, be it man, woman or horse."

Charms against toothache

At the time of the sacrament at mass, clench your teeth together and say the following:

"Os non comminutis ex eo."

Otherwise, another charm is as follows:

"Strigiles falseq denatae, dentium dolorem personate; O horse combs and sickles that have so many teeth, come heal me now of my toothache."

Against the falling evil or epilepsy

The following written charm, is taken from Reginald Scots disoverie of witchcraft. It makes use of the three wise men or Magi that gifted Jesu with Gold, frankincense, and myrrh. Their names are: Gasper, Melchior, and lastly Balthazar. The charm is said to have been presented to Pope Leo of Rome by an angel. It was said to be a true copy of holy writing given from God, in which Pope Leo then gave it to King Charles before he went into battle. The charm is said that they who recite three Pater Nosters (Lord's prayer) Three Aves (Hail Marys) and one Credo (apostles' creed) and carry this written prayer around with them shall not that day be overcome by their enemies either bodily or spiritually. It is said they will be mostly covered from a lot of misfortune such as: robbed or slain from thieves, pestilence, thunder/ lightening, hurt with fire/water, being hurt or harmed by faery folk, or any other falling evil. The written charm goes as such:

89

"*Gasper fert myrrham, thus Melchior, Balthasar aurum, Haec tria qui secum portabit nomina regum Solvitur a morbo Christi pietate caduco. Gasper with his myrrh began, these presents to unfold, Then Melchior brought in frankincense, And Balthasar brought in gold. Now he that of these holy kings the names about you bare, the falling evil by grace of Christ shall never need to fear. (check the evil: yll?)*"

That someone will sleep well

Write this prayer and put it beneath the head of the sufferer:

"*Oh Lord Jesus Christ, Father Almighty, who made the seven sleepers Maximinianus, Malcus, Martianus, Dionysis, John, Constantine, and Seraphion to sleep on Mount Sillion, be pleased to make this your servant (Name) rest in sleep, so that by your mercy he may obtain health of body and soul and praise you for ever. Amen.*"

-The Cambridge Book of Magic

Adding to this, some natural herbal remedies a person can use for insomnia is also lemon balm tea and Valerian tea. Be warned Lemon balm tea is more pleasant to drink than valerian, as valerian really does pack a punch in terms of scent.

To Help a woman deliver a child

According to Reginald scots discoverie, a way to bring about a speedy delivery for those with child who are overdue, would be to tie their girdle or shoelaces onto a church bell and strike it three times. This is said to bring about the child with great haste.

Charming a Bruise

Taken from Sarah Hewitt's book known as Nummits and Crummits: Devonshire customs, Characteristics and folklore is the following charm containing barbarous words is used in order to cure a bruise:

"Holy Chicha! Holy Chicha!

This bruise will go well by-and-bye.

Up sun high! Down moon low!

This bruise will be quite well very soon!

In the name of the father, son and holy Ghost

Amen!"

Healing Cage

the following text by Cecil Williamson in the museum of witchcraft and magic in Boscastle, describes what's known as a healing cage and its functions of healing. The cage could hold whatever items you desired that linked it towards that person, their full names, statements of intentions, bible verses or psalms for healing, I've seen spells like this that act as holders for a person's healing, to be very effective. They can later be put by the afflicted, or even burnt if the afflicted is further away, whilst the practitioner utters benedictions their way.

Text by Cecil Williamson from the museum of witchcraft and magic in Boscastle: *'Witches in Devon and Cornwall make their charms and spells from the gifts of wild nature growing naturally in field, hedge and wood. So, it is with this elongated twig container, bound either end and containing a compilation of moss, herbs, flower heads and seed pods, dried, prepared and spirit blessed. Purpose? In this instance to help a person recover from A serious fall from a horse causing back and internal injury.'*

A talisman for the Vapours

This charm was created by Cunning man of Chichester James Hallett in 1791. The cunning man had a handbill showing that he was well versed in herbal lore, astronomy, physic knowledge and could cast a horoscope to un-bewitch the enchanted, also advertising that he could draw up nativities for witchcraft. *"Great news to the afflicted!"* it read and claimed to be the original curer of all diseases. The charm itself was used for what was known as 'the vapours' meaning mental affliction in general. This covered a wide variety of ailments such as depression, dizziness, anxiety, hysteria, ect. This charm was in written form in an embroidery sampler, which was later replaced by a 1950s embroidery case and it read:

"Lord be praised this 20th day of June, 1791, was cured of the vapours my dear sister Miranda, cured by the help of God, and the curer of all ills, James Hallett."

Perhaps this exact charm could be utilised with the client's name and the date within it, alongside the use of medicine and treatments if they are prescribed by their GP or alongside counselling or other methods used. As a disclaimer, I would say anybody experiencing any form of mental health issues, should seek help. Consult with a GP and reach out to friends. Found in the Horniman museum and gardens.

Nettle Stings

When one is stung by a nettle, take a dock leaf, and rub the part affected saying:

> *"Nettle in, Dock out*
> *Dock in, Nettle out*
> *Nettle in, Dock out*
> *Dock rub, Nettle out."*

-Consult the oracle

Curing cattle with a penny and bread

In Reginald Scots discoverie, there is mention of an old woman that used to heal diseases in cattle who only ever took a penny and a loaf as payment. She had said that after she had touched the poorly creature, she departed immediately saying:

> *"My loaf in my lap,*
> *My penny in my purse*
> *Thou art never the better,*
> *And I am never the worse."*

Of use of thread and illness

Thread and its uses within British folk magic can be found all over the land within different areas of the UK throughout history. The multiple of uses with thread and its powers and influence for various cures and ailments in folk magic vary greatly. Included here are different methods and examples where they have been found to be utilised by cunning folk and charmers throughout history.

Taking the measure refers to the use of incorporating string, thread, or a piece of clothing, to divine illness or ailments in people whilst also being able to cure those certain ailments via the use of thread. In 1566 a cunning woman name Elizabeth Mentlock from Cambridge, done exactly this and confessed to diagnosing illness by measuring a band or girdle worn by the patient. The piece of clothing was measured from the elbow to the thumb and if the band was shorter and the cubit reached further than it normally did, then a diagnosis was given that the patient was suffering ill health through supernatural means. In witchcraft and second sight in the highlands and islands of Scotland, there exists a charm known as 'the gospel of Christ' which was performed on a Thursday or Sunday and spoken for healing. A green string kept in the conjurors mouth whilst the charm was uttered and then later secured to the patient's shoulder. The charm went as follows:

"*May God bless your cross before you go to any garden, any disease that is in it may he take from it. May god bless your crucifying cross, on top of a house, the house of christ, from drowning, from danger, and from fever. When the king of the three hills and a brown branch top ...(unintelligible)... may god bless what is before thee. When thou goest at their head success at* meeting and in battle; the grace of god and cureteous look of all men be yours; the banners of christ be over thee to protect thee from thy crown to thy sole. Fire will not burn thee, seas will not drown thee; a rock at sea art thou, a man on land art thou, fairer than the swan on loch lathaich, and the sea-gull on the white stream; you will rise above them as the wave rises, on the side of god and his powers. Thou art the red rowan tree to cause the wrath of men to ebb like a wave from the sea to flood tide, and a wave from flood tide to ebb.'

Witches in Boscastle and around other parts of the UK would sell knotted cord to sailors that When unbound, would raise, and stir winds. With this idea in mind, if wind was caught within the cord, then why not ill health? In Lancashire a string of nine knots was made and worn around the neck of a child to cure them of whooping cough. Within Scotland, a native of Uist claimed that red thread known as the 'Snaithnean' which was a woollen red thread around four to five inches long used to cure the evil eye that had been placed upon cattle. The wise person was said to say some good words over it, and it was given to the cattle to be tied around their tail to work its powers and influence over the cattle. There was also the idea of the wresting thread within Scotland too particularly when they were utilised to cure Sprains and fevers. A man in Yell, Shetland had a fever and could not sleep so a woman named Barbara stood in detling gave him a wresting thread with instructions the thread had to be wound about his head for the next nine nights and then burnt. Another variation is when a person had suffered a sprain the wresting thread would be cast upon them, it was in this reference seen as a thread spun from black wool and nine knots would be tied onto the afflicted area of the sprain. Whilst it was being put on the operator of the charm would mutter the following words unable to be heard fully by the client with the sprain:

The lord rode,

And the foul slipped,

He lighted

And she righted,

Set joint to joint

Bone to bone

And sinew to sinew

Heal in the Holy ghosts name!!!

    A very well-known and simple spell found within the areas of wart charming and ridding oneself of warts is to tie a string of the number of warts a person has, rubbing each knot with each wart and burying the string at a crossroads. Always keeping to the maxim of walking away and not looking back, in order to avoid undoing the working. Andro man would make cords where the patient would walk through the loop and after he would make a cat walk through the loop thus carrying the idea that the illness was transferred to the animal rather than remaining with the human.

    This isn't a new thing that hasn't been seen through the ages in British folk magic when it comes to transferral magic or 'contagion' as it is known for instance in the case of witch circles which were known to be drawn by ill wishing witches outside victim's houses.I t was said that victims would cross through them, thus gathering up the maledictions. If random circles suddenly appeared in somebodies farm, a poor unsuspecting animal would be made to walk through this firstly so that instead of the targeted victim, so that it would be the animal who gathered up the evil rather than the intended target of the spell. Lastly, on the subject of contagion within folk magic and basing this from older ideas and praxis, we could use a thread and tie it on a certain area around the body that is suffering the ailments such as a leg whilst repeating a certain charm or invocation upon it in order to transfer the ailment to the thread in whatever manner we feel comfortable, and then to tie a knot within it. Thus 'knotting in' the ailment and then tying it to a tree or looping it around a sapling, to transfer the ailment asking the tree or the spirit of the tree to accept the ailment in return giving an offering or libation to the tree.

To prevent Sea sickness

Saffron according to witchcraft detected, was a good cure against sea sickness and was to be suspended in a bag over the stomach.

To Cure Headaches

A most certain cure of headaches according to Egyptian secrets, and the magus is to take a herb growing out of the head of a statue and with it being bound or hung up with red thread will soon cure the violent pain.

In Consult the oracle, if you wear a snake's skin around your head, you will never suffer from the headache.

To cure whooping cough

In Essex, a charm to get rid of the whooping cough involved the patient crawling through a bramble or somebody being passed underneath the brambles several times as the following charm was said:

> *In bramble out cough,*
> *Here I leave the whooping cough.*

G.F Northall English folk rhymes 1892

To cure Bruises or Pain

I have performed this charm on a friend for period pain and it worked very well. Taking your hands, lay them upon the area that is affected (head for headache/lower stomach for period pain ect) and repeat the following charm three times:

> *Bruise/Pain thou shalt not heat,*
> *Bruise/Pain thou shalt not sweat,*
> *Bruise/Pain thou shalt not run*
> *No more than the Virgin Mary shall have another child.*

-Egyptian secrets Albertus Magnus

Teething

"The Vicar of a village in east Sussex was rather surprised the other day by one of his most respectable parishioners telling him that she never had any trouble with her children teething. Directly the moment her children showed any signs of it she borrowed a neighbour's donkey, set the child backwards on the cross of the

donkey's neck, and led it while she repeated the Lord's prayer, and she never had any more trouble."

The idea of donkeys having power is not a one-off thing when it comes to folk magic. However, when it comes to aspects of Christian folk magic, it's become a well-known factor as the tale goes that the donkey rode Mary who was pregnant with the saviour to the inn. Ever since then it bore a cross on its back, I have known people to snip a small bit of hair from the middle of the cross on a donkey's back and utilise this in folk healing charms for the prior reason mentioned.

consult the oracle: a Victorian guide to folklore and fortune telling.

A general remedy

To fan the patient with the leaves taken out of a bible will go a long way in covering curing a lot of ailments.

Consult the oracle 1899

Anaemia

For this condition, there stands a simple remedy. A couple of drops of the patients' blood is buried underneath a rose bush to help have 'ruddy cheeks'

Consult the Oracle

To Cure Fever

Take an earthenware pot and it is to be filled with a lock of the patient's hair, their nail and toe clippings and a raw piece of beef. A black silk cloth is then to be tied over the mouth of the vessel. The charm is then buried in a remote forest where it is best left undisturbed. The idea being, as the meat rots away so does the patient's fever.

-Michael Howards East Anglian Witches and Wizards

A charm for the Shingles

Taken from a folk tale from the Welsh fairy Book, the following charm describes a simple method from a conjuror named Huw Llwyd who was said to be a seventh son of a seventh son and thus denoting him a conjurer naturally. All they had to do was to spit on the rash and say:

> *"Male eagle, female eagle, I send you over nine seas, and over nine mountains, and over nine acres of waste land, where no dog shall bark and no cow shall low, and no eagle shall higher rise "--which is quite simple."*

Huw Llwyd was also said to have eaten eagles' flesh so that Nine generations of his family would be able to charm away the shingles. Eagles are now unfortunately an endangered species so perhaps just stick to chicken!

To stop the flow of Blood

"In the blood of Adam death was taken,

In the blood of Christ it was also shaken,

And by the same blood I do the charge

That thou do run no longer at large."

-witchcraft detected and prevented

To Cure those with breathing problems

This charm I have used on animals and people alike that have suffered from severe breathing problems and difficulties. I found the inspiration from a charm which is originally a famous toothache spell involving Jesus passing by St Peter with toothache and healing him (the actual spoken charm is supplied in the charm: To transfer the toothache.) but modified it to the following cause. Take a large Hag stone and run a bath. Make sure the hole in the stone is large enough so that the water may pass freely through it. Keep focus here seeing the person/animal starting to breath properly then repeat the following and build up a chant seeing the water running into the bath turning white with light:

One day our Lord rode by and stumbled across a Person/animal who could not breath, what ails thee? Said our Lord. For I cannot breathe replied the creature/Person. Then arise said Our Lord, arise and ye be healed arise and yes shall breathe freely!

Keep this chant going over and over and then allow the person to have the bath.

For corporal or spiritual rest

In nominee patris, up and down,

Et filli and spiritus sancti upon my crown,

Crux Christi upon my breast,

Sweet lady, send me eternal rest!

Reginald scots

The sacred heart: spells of Love, favour, and Success

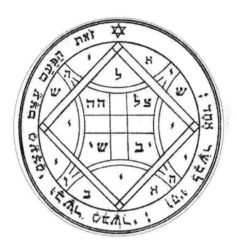

The 4th pentacle of Venus taken from the seals of Solomon

To Stop infidelity in a partner

In performing this modern spell, take a padlock and a key along with some of your and your partners personal effects. In the base of the padlock where it is shut down and locked, input these personal effects and proceed to baptise the padlock with some holy water and say:

In nominee et patris et filli et spirit santu I baptise thee (full name) just like this padlock may you never come undone nor want for anybody else and commit yourself whole heartedly only for me, may it be I who only holds the key to your heart and body. May your loins

be locked for others and unlocked only for me that holds the key Fiat Fiat Fiat!

Lock the padlock and putting it into a bucket of water by your partners threshold. As the water rusts the metal fuses the padlock, so your partner will not want for anybody else. Keep the key close to you and in a safe place where your partner will not find it.

Love Divination by the new moon

When a country girl see's the new moon after midsummer, she should go to a stile, turn her back against it and say:

> All hail, new moon, all hail to thee!
> I prithee, good moon, reveal to me
> This night who shall my true love be;
> Who he is and what he wears,
> And what he does all months and years.

You will see an apparition of your future partner.

Consult the oracle

To gain the love of a woman

To gain the love of a woman, this charm taken by reginal Scots discoverie gives the idea of working with wax and fire to bring about a desired female towards you: To obtain a woman's love, an image must be made from virgin wax in the hour of Venus, in the name of the person you wish to influence. A character is also inscribed upon the image itself and it is then left to be warmed at a fire and as this warms the name of an angel must be mentioned. There are once again no characters inputted here in this charm, but from the Venusian nature one can only assume that the characters inscribed are astrological characters based on Venus. The angel of Venus is also known as Haniel. Considering this, I have inputted an astrological symbol of Venus:

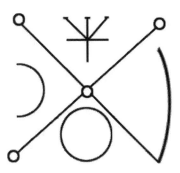

To remove disorder between husband and wife

A Loadstone carried by a man will remove disorder between a husband and wife.

Witchcraft detected.

My Mothers Sweetening spell

An effective spell to sweeten a person up is to write their full name clearly, placing it at the bottom of a sugar pot. I found out about this when I was round my mothers, and my brother randomly questioned:

"What's Tina doing at the bottom of the sugar pot?" My mum replied with: *"Put the Bitch back, she's not sweet enough yet."*

The even Ash leaf charm

The following four lines are to be used by those anxious of their future in love. They must gather an even ash leaf, and hold it in their hand walk along the road saying:

This even ash I carry in hand,
The first I meet shall be my husband!
If he be single let him draw nigh,
But if he be married then he may pass by.

To ensure success, the leaf is sometimes thrown at the passer by.

Consult the oracle

If you come Before a Judge

If you wish to have the love and favour of any worshipful man (a man in power.) write his name and his mother's name binding it underneath your right armpit and carry it with you and you shall have his love. If you want to have what you desire and have to ask a worthy man, then write the following in parchment and hang it on your right arm:

O God give the King my judgement.

You are to also say this as often as possible.

-The Cambridge book of magic.

To Gain Favour from those around you

To gain love of great people carry Vervain about thee

-Grimoire of Arthur gauntlet

In the Grimoire of Arthur Gauntlet also known as sloane MS3851 which is edited by David Rankine. It is said that for a person to gain favour of those around them, they must carry the enchanters herb Vervain about them. One way we can adapt this is by use of the clothing we wear. In this modern world whether it be social gatherings such as weddings, christenings, Bar/Bat Mitzvahs, Funerals or even business and corporate events, a useful way for the modern practitioner to carry the herb Vervain around them is to place some of the dried herb into a small paper bag and make a small package then to sow it into the back of a tie. Within British folk magic there seems to be some mention of charms that involve the person sowing in charms into items of clothing, such as sowing a herring's bone into an enemy's clothes to bring about death. the idea that by sowing these charms into clothing, they bring the desired influences to a person by literally becoming the garments on their back. Also, with the act of sowing it shows that we are literally sowing into those garments our will and desire. Interestingly, there seems to be a number of magical methods from cunning folk and grimoires alike. I have in the past used this method of utilising vervain in order to gain favour in social situations. Admittedly from personal experience, I have harvested the plant itself, but I have also made use of the plant in dried store-bought form and just spoken to the plant itself before it being sowed it into a tie.

To make a Lover return

To make a lover return from a journey, a person must secretly put common clover in their shoe.

-Consult the oracle

To gain love of somebody

For gaining the love of somebody you desire, take an apple, writing the following words upon it:

Coamer, synady, huepide

Then holding the apple in both hands speak the following conjuration:

I conjure thee apple, by these three names written on thee, that whosoever shall eat thee shall burn in my love

Then feed the apple to the one you wish to bewitch. There's no reason why in these modern times we can't actually use the apple to make some sort of cake for somebody. In terms of believability, I feel somebody would rather eat free cake than a free apple!

A True Love Powder

Taken from witchcraft detected and prevented, this curious recipe calls for putting a mixture into somebody's drink and is said to work wonderful effects to your advantage. However, the recipe calls for mistletoe berries which are extremely poisonous if ingested. A good alternative to the usage of this powder is to create a talisman with your name along with the person's name joining from a common letter and the person's personal affects within it with the powder and carried about in a charm bag.

The recipe states as such: *take elecampane (also known as horse heal or elf dock) the seeds and dowers of vervain, and the berries of mistletoe, dry them well in an oven, and beat them into a fine powder (give the party you desire upon a dram of wine.)*

The Burning of salt to bring love

A very effective but simplistic method that reiterates how much in folk magic we utilise what we have around us, calls for two very simple ingredients: Open Fire and Salt. The spell goes as such:

It is not this salt I wish to burn, it is my lovers heart to turn, that he may not rest nor happy be, until he comes and speaks to me

A good thing I would recommend, would be to build this up as a chant whilst holding the salt in your hand and visualising the intended person coming forward to you, building the chant up and up and to then throw it into the fire. This spell has to be done for three consecutive Fridays- the day of the planet Venus. I would even further argue that performing the spell in the hour of Venus also will help amplify its power by bringing more Venusian intelligences into the conjuration. The original conjuration itself calls for salt and fire and is taken from the book the hand of destiny by **CJS Thompson**, the rest in regard to the planetary hours are recommendations by myself.

The Plucking of Yarrow to cause him to come

Go to the grave of a young man where yarrow grows from and pluck it out of the grave, as you do so say:

Yarrow, sweet yarrow, the first that I have found, And in the name of Jesus, I pluck it from the ground, As Joseph loved sweet Mary, and took her for his dear, So in a dream this night, I hope my true love will appear.

The Yarrow is then placed underneath the person's pillow

-Consult the oracle

The Slow Burner Heart and Pins spell

This charm I concocted for a client, and it had some very powerful and interesting results! The spell is used to bring a loved one back where there has been separation, quarrel and discord. The influence I got from this spell, was originally from the heart and pins spell we see in British folk magic. This is where an animal would become bewitched and die, and so the heart would be taken out of the corpse and driven with pins, shards of glass, nails and then normally inputted by the side of the chimney so as the heart shrinks and the pins heat, it will then diminish the powers of the witch casting the maleficia. Not only this, but another influence was also the burning of salt spell inputted in this book to cause a person to come towards you in a romantic way.

This spell goes more sympathetic in the sense the heart represents the heart of the person that you're wishing to influence with otherworldly powers to bring them back to you. On a Friday, go and buy yourself a lamb's heart from the butchers without haggling over the price. Then you make an insertion into the heart and input into it a photograph of you both together, and the desired persons personal effects, this could involve their hair, nails, semen or sexual fluids (very potent in this particular type of working). The incision is then to be sowed up with a needle and thread, and then the nails are driven into the heart as the words are spoken:

It is not this heart I wish to prick but the heart of (full name) I wish to prick, may then not eat, nor sleep, nor rest, nor be until that they come back to me.

As each pin or nail that is inputted into the heart the following spell is recited over and over. The heart is now put into the oven and slowly roasted. As this happens, continue reciting the charm seeing them drawing towards you and making contact. The heart is to be partly roasted and placed in foil on a plate in a place where it will not be interrupted. Every day for the next seven days, the heart is to be part roasted again and taken out and the following chant is repeated as it slowly roasts. The idea of this being that as the heart burns and heats, so does the heart of the intended target. Once the following Friday comes, you must venture to a cemetery to find the grave of a married couple. The heart is then buried as well as suitable offerings such as flowers, fresh water, incense, vigil lights, memorial candles to be given to the spirits of that grave to not anger them and cause havoc on your spell. After burying the heart, walk away and do not look back.

You may make use of a piece of Clover

Another charm to be used by young men and maidens who wish to know their future spouses, the following is used. The 'clover of two' means a piece of clover with only two leaves upon it.

A clover, a clover of two,
Put it in your right shoe,
The first young man (or woman) you meet,
field, in street, in lane,
You'll have him/her or one of his/her name.

Consult the oracle

A charm to thwart and remove a run of bad luck

Ever have it when no matter what you seem to do there is always something, always an obstacle and no matter how much you remove the other obstacle, there only ever seems to be another more arduous task in its space? This modern charm was originally utilised to remove bad luck in a family, it was something that I had created as no matter what happened there seemed to always be this string (more like a rope) of bad luck over and over again.

The charm itself is easy. Find yourself a large stone, the bigger the better. Then with your stone, take yourself to a large body of water, whilst holding the stone project into it all the bad luck that has been occurring there is also a chant that can be combined with this:

Creature of earth, creature of stone
Take bad luck from house and home.

Chant repeatedly, keeping this motion going until you feel that bad luck is fully imbued into that stone. Then take your hands and speak to the stone, telling it how you are removing the bad luck from that household into the body of water. As you throw it say loudly with intention:

FIAT FIAT FIAT!

Walk away, don't look back and tell nobody who wasn't there of your workings that evening.

To Gain a promotion in your work

On a Thursday the day of Jupiter, take yourself some green thin and workable leather, a needle and thread and sow yourself a small pouch with an entry way to input items. Get yourself a small leather strip to tie the bag shut with. Gather the following plants: Clover/Shamrock and Heather for luck, Cinquefoil which is commonly known as five finger grass, which in the Egyptian secrets advises that it be carried around when wanting to gain favour from others higher up than you. Each time you cut the plants off, make sure you take the time to commune with the spirit of the plant asking if you may harvest its beautiful plants (flattery and good manners will get you everywhere) and in return you'll give the spirit an offering. This offering can be a libation of milk, coins, butter, alcohol, but above all make sure what you're libating to the plant wont actually harm it in some way, as that will be counterproductive.

Another item to get is some dirt gathered from inside a horseshoe imprint on the ground for strength in your position at your workplace. With this you can get creative in the sense of what you will be adding into it objects associated with Luck such as a fingers crossed pendant, a mini lucky horseshoe, a lucky rabbits foot, the world really is your oyster. Another herb to add to this is Fenugreek as this is a great plant for acquiring good luck and if need be, you acquire it in any supermarket or greengrocers. I realise ive gone over a large number of items, but this is to encourage your own creativity making it your own. The bare minimum you'll need to acquire this charm is the clovers or shamrocks, fenugreek, five finger grass, Heather and your Hair. Then on a Sunday, perform the conjuration for Sunday asking the Spirits of the Sun to help bless and consecrate your charm as you craft it. Ask them for success and good fortune in getting a Promotion and moving forward in your job role and that they will grant you success and in return you'll give an offering for them of incense in their name. take the items and speak to each one of them whilst blessing them in a solar incense of your choosing, a popular choice is frankincense. Take each item through the smoke and input these objects into your green leather bag. Once this is done, tie the bag shut leaving the charm onto the characters of the sun drawn on the floor with liquid chalk along with a lit candle. The next day carry the talisman about with you in work.

When you're working too many hours in a job

Sadly, during this day and age sometimes working a job we're expected a lot of and there is a rise of people sacrificing their free time they have, limiting their time mainly to work. I've been there and it's not a good place to be, because of this becoming more and more frequent in modern society and having suffered it myself, I have designed the following charm that embodies the problems essence in an effigy so that you're able to convey your will over this. Firstly, obtain a personal effect of your target who is disturbing these hours to you, it could be their hair, nail clippings, spit, ect. Then take a good lump of clay and imbue the personal effects into the clay, and from it fashion yourself an image of what they look like, you don't have to be a Picasso, just try to mark out their face and features it needs to be recognisable for you, not nobody else.

Also, if there are any distinguishing features this person has such as a mole, one of their eyes may be distorted, craft it on the image. Shape them according to sex also if they are female give them breasts and a vagina, if they are female give them a penis and testicles, again its no exception in shaping the more intimate areas, this is folk magic there is no need to be prude here! If you know somebody has bigger boobs go big! If you know somebody has any scars or had surgeries, then shape it! Have they got a big penis and you've seen evidence? Shape that bad boy! I cannot stress it enough but make it as much like them, the more likeness here, the more accuracy. However, despite this raising the question of: George what in God's hell has your relationship been like with your previous employers?! It's more of a case attention to detail in folk magic. As this is being shaped, it is very important for you to keep constant focus of them in your minds eye.

Call out their full name repeating it over and over again the whole time as you craft this image. After the image has been made, take a piece of string or cord and tie nine knots into it, with each knot tie into it your will.

Similar to a way of working the witches' ladder in the curses and maledictions chapter. As each knot is tied, shout affirmatively your will into the open knot tying it shut fast, catching your intent into the knot. After nine knots have been tied, you are going to take your cord and wrap it tightly around the clay image. Sealing it into a final knot, as this knot is open you're going to speak to the image as if it were the one making you work these hours and talk to them. Tell them what you REALLY want to say. Be direct and be honest in what you want, and above all speak from your heart. Tell them how its making you feel and what effect it is having upon you and your life. In this section I can't tell you what you need to say as this comes from YOU, all the spells with verses in this book are advisory as you will know by this point and in matters of talking from your heart, its completely personal to YOU. After this has been said, tie the open knot fastening it three times in total. Take the image and make it face a corner of the wall, so it is unable to see anything else apart from your will and intent. Make sure the image will be left in a place where it is undisturbed, as you must realise with image magic what happens to the image will echo into that persons physical, reality so be very careful how you act with the image.

    Three further points to add to this conjuration, firstly, I want to add it is important that you actually go and speak to your superior in the mundane and structure a good professional conversation beforehand about the issue at hand. Be open and honest but professional. Unlike the approach of communication when speaking with the clay image which will be very different and more forceful. Secondly, if their not complying you can always strengthen the spell by wrapping the image round with brambles that have been blessed beforehand with your will and intent, use gloves and be careful as brambles are a hardy prickly plant.

Thirdly, as this working uses image magic as a means to deliver your will, it therefore means the clay image represents the person you're targeting, so treat this doll carefully. See it as a living embodiment of that person. It is important that after this spell has worked, take the image to a south flowing river, telling the image it has served its purpose and is no longer a representation of the person you intended it for. For instance:

"You are no longer a living breathing image of (full name) but only a creature made of clay, your purpose has been served and I completely cleanse you of this person's essence."

submerge the image under water speaking the person's name backwards as the clay will break away into the river, cleansing the image of the essence of the intended person.

Three Bee's Charm

Located in the museum of witchcraft and magic in Boscastle, exists a curious little charm consisting of three bee's placed in a leather blue bag designed to bring happiness, wealth and fortune, these creatures are said to only nest in harmonious locations. According to Cecil Williamson, this is his description and explanation of the charm:

'Some witch's charms are just draw string pouches with things stuffed inside. These are safe enough for a peep, but leave the sealed-up ones well alone. Always

remember that. Here we have three dear old bumble humble bees, put carefully in a blue leather pouch, and hung up out of the way in the best room in the house, they will bring health, happiness and sweet good fortune to this sun blessed spot. A widespread Devon charm, this one recovered in 1949 from Dawlish.'

Isle of Mann charm for a good fishing catch

Another of these charmers, who lived in Ballaugh, was specially noted for his skill in bringing luck in fishing to those who applied to him. One of these was told by the old fellow that he could not put the fish in their nests; but he could anything that might cause him to be unsuccessful. He then gave him a lot of herbs, which he was to pound and boil, and mix with a pint of whisky. Of this compound, a glass was first to be taken by the captain of the boat, and then by each man in it, and the rest was to be sprinkled over the boat and nets. On one occasion he was sent by his fellows, after a spell of ill luck in the fishing, to see the old charmer; but being somewhat sceptical, he spent the charmers fee on drink and compounded the nostrum himself; though quite ignorant of the proper herbs, the result was a magnificent haul that night; but he never dared tell his comrades of the trick he had played on them

.-Rhys Folklore of the Isle of Mann

An interesting point regarding what herbs one could use for this conjuration to bring the fish, could be taken from other magical workbooks to help list some ideas. However, what I will say is as always make sure the herbs and plants you're employing in your conjuration aren't poisonous and aren't going to harm you in any way. For instance, the following list of herbs/plants/ingredients was taken from a charm to bring fish to somebody from the Egyptian secrets of Albertus Magnus:

> *Valerian, Fish Berry or known also as levant nut and Indian berry, flour.*

Again, this is just an idea, I'm sure so that other plants can be used considering the second attempt actually worked for the man who compounded the mixture himself from random plants and herbs to save himself some money for beer!

Turning of change under the new moon

There is a Cornish charm in the conjuring of money under the new moon, where the person looks at the new moons silver increasing sliver whilst turning their money around in their pockets. Nowadays we tend to live in a more growing cashless society, and so turning a person debit card or credit card three times in their pocket whilst gazing at the new moon can also facilitate this.

Conjuring Money Via Rain Water

This charm makes use pf primarily 3 ingredients and is simple yet effective. It's not an old spell found in the 14th century, in fact its modern and was created by myself but ive found it so useful in acquiring money when payday is not even near. Firstly, take a bowl and gather rainwater, the harder and more dramatic the rain that fell, the more potent the spell as the idea is to call money so it rains down onto you.

Take some change, putting this into the bowl. Place your hands over the vessel of rain and change, then see it literally raining money down on you, really take your time to visualise this and push that intention into the bowl of water. If you have familiar spirits you work with you can call on them to aid you in this and to help empower your charm. Once this has been done take the water aspersing it from your front door, around each different room, leading to the back door. You could even create a chant of something simple such as:

Money to me, Money to me, Money to me.

This charm is something I have used and found such a great success rate with, and I thought I'd share it with you all. With the remaining left-over change, feel free to spend this and see that money coming back your way.

Alice Kytelers broom charm

Dame Alice Kyteler was one of Irelands first accused witches in the year of 1324. She was accused of witchcraft, as having her 4th husband pass away and get ill made gossip turn ugly as it was believed that she had acquired demonic help in order to gain her wealthy lifestyle. An interesting piece of information, is that her servant Petronella de meath after being whipped six times, confessed that Alice would sweep the dirt on the town's streets towards her son's house whilst muttering a spell that would bring all of the wealth from the town towards her son.

It could be an avid idea to do such a thing, although if you don't want to be seen on the streets with a broomstick sweeping and talking to yourself, the following modification may be better suited.

If you live in flats where the foyer is concrete what better thing to do than go from your neighbours houses to your own. Yes of course this is transferring wealth from them to you, but if you don't like your neighbours particularly well then, I'm sure this would work an absolute treat!

A French charm for gambling

The spell this book is taken from, is known as the grimoire of pope honourious. (not to be confused with the sworn book of honourious) It was a book that had a big influence and was used by cunning folk across France and unlike many other grimoires, the book of secrets at the back of the back which is simple folk charming and folk magic, is quite lengthy in comparison. This is a charm to win at games, firstly before sunrise, and on the eve of St Peter, you must gather the herb known as devils' bit but before this is done, the Characters presented have to be inscribed on the ground where it is gathered. Place it upon a rock that has been consecrated, for a day and then wait until it has dried. Reduce it to a powder and carry it with you.

To recover Lost Items

Burn a good handful of street dirt alongside a worn-out shoe, saying the *credo* prayer 3 times. Making the sign of the cross before and after the conjuration.

Credo in Deum Patrem omnipotentem, creatorem caeli et terrae. Et in Iesus Christum, Fillius eius unicum, Dominum nostrum, qui conceptus est de spiritu sancto, natus ex Maria Virgine, passus sub Pontio pilato, crucifixus, mortuus, et sepultus, descendit ad inferos, tertia die resurrexit a mortuis, ascendit ad caelos, sedet ad dexteram Dei patris omnipotentis, inde venturus est iudicare vivos et mortuos. Credo in spiritum sanctum, sanctam ecclesiam Catholicam, sanctorum communionem, remissionem peccatorum, carnis resurractionem, vitam aeternam.

Amen.

-The Black Dragon/ The crossed keys

The cunning man's arsenal:
Defence

The right spell for thieves

In the name of the father and of the son and of the hoy spirit amen.

Defend this my house ground and goods this night and all other times from all thieves, witches and also spirits elves and all other evils and I charge thee thou spirit that hast the charge especial of open as of secret things and by the virtue of the omnipotent power of Almighty God maker of heaven and earth and creator of all the mortal flesh and of secret things and by the virtue of the omnipotent power of almighty god maker of heaven and earth and creator of all mortal flesh and of all other things visible and invisible and I charge thee thou spirit by all the holy names of God the most highest + Elo Ely Sabaoth Adonay Saday Tetragrammaton Alpha et Omega and by all the names of God that may be spoken or not spoken also I remind *thee thou spirit which are called Banalum By all the aforesaid naming and by the virtue and power of them that if any thief or thieves hitherwards to me within this place where I go with my goods belonging to me or else also I charge thee Banalo by the great virtue and power of almighty God and the Virgin Mary Gods mother and by all the powers of St Peter and St Paul and by all the Holy company in heaven and by the angels and archangels that if any thief or thieves hitherwards come they may be struck down both blind and that still stand to or they are kept as stiff as any staff!'*

-Grimoire of Arthur Gauntlet

To 'Spoil' a theif, a witch, or any other enemy and to be delivered from the evil.

On a Sunday Morning before sunrise, cut a wand of Hazel whilst saying the following spell:

I cut thee o bough of this summers growth, inn the name of him/her whom I mean to beat and maim.

Then take a cloth, and cover a table and state the following:

In Nomine patris + & filli +& spiritus sancti +ter.

Then saying:

Drochs myroch, esenaroth + betu + baroch + ass +maaroth. Holy Trinity punish him/her that hath wrought this mischief and take away by great justice Eson + Elion + emaris, ales, age.

Then strike the cloth with the hazel wand. A point I may add is that it may be best repeatedly striking the cloth envisioning it as the intended thief/witch receiving those inflictions.

-Reginald Scots Discovery of witchcraft.

An old charm Against House Fire

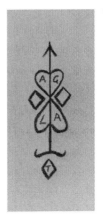

This book is primarily aimed at British folk magic; however, our European brothers and sisters have had influences over the development of British folk magic through different texts such as Agrippas four books of occult philosophy which is one of the foundations of the western magical traditions. There was a charm found in the northern Netherlands in 1909, which was an oyster shell containing a sigil drawn onto it spelling the names of AGLA one of the sacred names of God. The name itself is actually a cabalistic acronym meaning: *You Oh Lord are mighty forever.*" In the book the most holy trinosophia, a French esoteric book dated in the late 18th century, the name AGLA was responsible for preserving Lot and his family from the fire of the abrahamic cities Sodom and Gomorrah. The neighbouring cities themselves were said to be consumed by fire and brimstone. There is also the idea that the oyster itself representing the element of water and AGLA being spelt upon it to put the influence of God lending his protection upon a family and threshold through fire upon that charm.

Exorcism of the evil eye

I trample upon the eye, As tramples the duck upon the lake, as tramples the swan upont he water, as tramples the horse upon the plain, as tramples the cow upon the 'uic' as tramples the host of the elements. Power of wind have I over it, power of wrath have I over it, power of fire have I over it, power of thunder have I over it, power of lightening have I over it, power of storms have I over it, power of moon have I over it, power of sun have I over it, power of stars have I over it, power of firmament I have over it, power of the heavens and of the worlds I have over it, power of the heavens and of the words I have over it. A portion of it upon the grey stones, a portion of it upon the steep hills, a portion of it upon the fast falls, a portion of it upon the fair meads, and a portion upon the great salt sea, the best instrument to carry it. In the name of the three of life, in the name of the sacred three, in the name of all the secret ones, and of the powers together."

Inputted here is also the Gàidhlig variation:

Saltraim air an t-suil, Mar a shaltrais lach air luin, Mar a shaltrais eal air burn, Mar a shaltrais each air uir, Mar a shaltrais earc air iuc, Mar a shaltrais feachd nan dul, Mar a shaltrais feachd nan dul. Ta neart gaoith agam air, Ta neart fraoich agam air, Ta neart teine agam air, Ta neart torruinn agam air, Ta neart dealain agam air, Ta neart gaillinn agam air, Ta neart gile agam air, Ta neart greine agam air, Ta neart nan reul agam air, Ta neart nan speur agam air, Ta neart nan neamh Is nan ce agam air, Neart nan neamh Is nan ce agam air. Trian air na clacha glasa dheth, Trian air na beanna casa dheth, Trian air na h-easa brasa dheth, Trian air na liana maiseach dheth, 'S trian air a mhuir mhoir shalach, 'S i fein asair is fearr gu ghiulan, A mhuir mhor shalach, Asair is fearr gu ghiulan. An ainm

Tri nan Dul, An ainm nan Tri Numh, An ainm nan uile Run, Agus nan Cursa comhla.

-Carmina Gadelica

For a thing which has been stolen

Write down all the names of the suspected thieves on pieces of paper and then put each person's name into a ball of clay, putting them all into a vessel of Holy Water. (I see of no reason why you cannot fill the vessel with unblessed water and then pour into it after a couple of drams of holy water.) Then say the following Orison:

I conjure you Holy water by the Father, the son, and the Holy Spirit and by St Mary the mother of our Lord Jesus Christ, and by heaven and earth and sun and moon, and by fire and water and by all that is in Heaven and on Earth and in Sea, by the angels and archangels, by thrones and dominions, and by the four evangelists Matthew, Mark, Luke and John and by the four rivers of paradise dividing this earth in three or four parts; and send up the name who is responsible, to the praise of Christ.

Amen

The name of the suspected thief should reveal itself and float.

-The Cambridge book of magic

To Compel a thief to return stolen property

The grimoire this charm is taken from is Albertus Magnus Egyptian secrets: white and black arte for man and beast. The use for this grimoire by British cunning folk, was used more recently as the English translation for it was published in 1914. In Joyce Froomes book Wicked enchantments, she mentions a charm carried around by expatriate St Lucian cunning men which protects against thieves:

> *Mary toiled and bore the child; three angels were her nurses. The first is named Saint Michael, the others name Saint Gabriel the third is Saint Peter. Three thieves' approach to steal the child of Mary; Mary spoke, Saint Peter bind. Saint peter said: I have bound it with Iron fetters, with Gods own hands that they must stand like a stick and look like a buck until they are able to count all the stars all the rain drops that fall into the ocean all grains of sand fro and to it they cannot do this they must and with my tongue can bid them to arise and order them to go without ado thus I forbid the thieves my own my all and make the thief repent and fall +++ give the thief three times strokes and bid him depart hence in the name of the Lord.*

This of course is not to get confused with the grimoire named the secrets of Albertus magnus: of the virtue of herbs, stones and certain beasts, also a book of marvels of the world. These two grimoires were published in very different times. The secrets being published in the sixteenth century in around 1650, whilst the Egyptian secrets appearing in 1725. These books aren't related as many would assume. The term: Egyptian secrets was not to indicate this was magic from the Egyptian people. Rather than, it meant the Romany gypsy people.

Egyptian secrets however was used by cunning folk in America, and also by those who practiced

Braucheri or what's known as Pow Wow, other grimoire favoured also by these folk practices were the 6th and 7th book of moses. In regard to Braucheri, this system of folk magic is derived from the Pennsylvanian Dutch settlers in America, the practices of Braucheri are extremely similar to the practices of its British cousin. They are not the same tradition and I want to make that perfectly clear, but they do hold similarities such as the idea of contagion, charming burns, cattle charming, the similar beliefs on witches and unbewitching services they would provide, the use of the SATOR SQUARE, the Abracadabra talisman, and other variations of that, I found this charm in Egyptian secrets and I must say I found it very interesting indeed.

Obtain a new Earthernware pot with a cover, draw the water under the current of a stream whilst calling out the three highest names:

"In the name of the father, the son and the holy spirit."

Fill the vessel one-third, take the same to your home and set it upon the fire, take a piece of bread from the lower crust of the loaf, stick 3 pins into the bread, boil it all in the vessel, add a few dew nettles and say:

"Thief male or female bring my stolen articles back, whether thou art boy or girl, thief if thou art woman or man, I compel thee in the name of the father the son and holy ghost amen."

Cross yourself three times.

A Charm to drive away spirits that haunt any house

Take Virgin Parchment paper, making four equal pieces, on each piece of paper writing the words:

Omnis Spiritus Laudet Dominum: Mosen habent & prophetas: Exurgat Deus et dissipentur inimici ejus.

Hang this in the four corners of your house.

-Reginald Scots discoverie

To Bless a Hag Stone with Protective Virtues

A hag stone or a Holed Stone will carry protective virtues naturally, however sometimes it is always good to charge things with intent in order to amplify their spirit force and power. A good method is to go into a catholic church and go to the Holy water basins used to anoint followers before they enter. There take your hag stone, including the necklace and drop it into the water and cross yourself saying:

In Nomine Patris et Filli et Spiritus Sancti

lay your hands over it. Repeat the following Charm:

I baptise thee creature of Stone, be thou sained and imbued with the powers of protection, protect me from all harm, all accidents, all injuries and all bewitchments this I pray in the name of the father, son and holy spirit Amen

Fiat Fiat Fiat!

Take the stone out of the vessel and use it for your purposes.

Drawing of Blood to Destroy the Evil Eye

Many of the 'human charms' are/were used on animals and vice versa.

-Graham King British book of charms and spells

When cattle were overlooked or had thought to have been *tudded*, one of the many remedies performed was to draw blood from the ill wished animal, letting it spill upon some hay. The hay would then be burnt in a fire, seeing the blood being linked to the one who had cast the evil eye upon the unfortunate animal. I would not recommend drawing blood purposely from an animal you believe has been ill wished as this could make them even more ill. I would also hate the thought that somebody had performed this charm from this book and seriously hurt or injured an animal unless the animal had drawn blood by some accidental means. However, in a lot of cases cattle charming and human charming could be interchanged. So, in turn a remedy for being overlooked would be for the afflicted to draw blood from yourself and spill it upon some hay and burn it upon a fire. I would further add here to evaluate the smoke and the patterns it makes to divine who the perpetrator was or what tools or methods they had used to bewitch you.

The Art of Reduction

If we look at the ways some cunning folk worked in terms of the charms and operations used, we can see that a lot of their magic involves the use of reduction here so for

instance the famous ABRACADABRA spell which
means I create when I speak, often diminishes in spelling:

ABRACADABRA
ABRACADABR
ABRACADAB
ABRACADA
ABRACAD
ABRACA
ABRAC
ABRA
ABR
AB
A

Forming a downward triangle like this could represent the actual ailment or illness itself diminishing incorporating that sympathetic element that a lot of folk magic has utilised. It was normally worn around a patient's neck in a charm bag or surrounded by a piece of fabric sown around it. So, with that in mind, perhaps we ourselves could utilise this element of reduction magic? Its powerful indeed so imagine if we were to do exactly the same with the name of an illness. After all, to know somethings name is to have power over it and if we know what illness it is then with this formula of reduction magic, we ourselves could utilise this for instance:

EARACHE
EARACH
EARAC
EARA
EAR
EA
E

There is no limit here in a sense to what we can't reduce, if we're thinking in terms of bewitchment how to diminish the power the witch holds over their victim, then once we have the witches actual name and we know for sure who it is, perhaps we could write the witches full name and diminish it? Perhaps putting the suspected witches name in a bag filled with Trefoil, St John's Wort, Vervain, and Dill which was said to hinder witches of their will, could take away and decrease the powers of the suspected ill-wisher. These are modern forms of praxis based upon older form of practice but again very applicable to the times now and still carries forward that element of reduction:

SARAHBARNS
SARAHBARN
SARAHBAR
SARAHBA
SARAHB
SARAH
SARA
SAR
SA
S

For Protection upon a foot journey and ensure you don't get easily tired

A modern charm created by myself to ensure that protection is given on a walked journey. Gather the dirt out of the footprint of a horse with an iron horseshoe, and hold it in a bag with the following written in a piece of paper:

AGLA   AGLA

> *" St George he rode, upon the horses back,*
> *Trampling upon Evil and Dragons, Trampling upon thieves,*
> *Trampling upon witches, trampling upon tired and weariness,*
> *trampling upon goblins, trampling upon accidents,*
> *Let his horse guide me upon this journey*
> *And keep me free from harm,*
> *Let his horse guide me upon this journey,*
> *And keep my soul at ease."*
> FIAT   FIAT   FIAT

AGLA   AGLA

The charm should be kept in your right shoe. Iron will keep you safe from all harm, and the strength of the horse will keep you strong.

Aspersing with Rowan and Water

The famous Rowan tree is known throughout British folk magic for its powerful protective properties against evils spirits, witchcraft, and ill-wishing. Has typically been used by threading onto a red thread, its scarlet red berries coming from the term: *"rowan berries and red thread puts all warlocks to their speed."* Its wood has also been used to make rowan crosses, which would be tied to cattle or hung up in stables to protect them against being afflicted by the evil eye. In this instance, however, the following new charm makes the use of rowan sprigs and water as a means to counteract and send away any evil eye that has befallen the client.

To begin with, in the springtime venture to a rowan tree and speak to it. Ask the tree if you can use some of its sprigs to use in a charm to send away evil, asking for its spirit to bless those sprigs with its protective virtues. Leave an offering to the tree, this can be a coin, a libation a milk, some food such as bread, butter, cheese or some of your blood. Take the sprig home and have a vessel of water collected from a sacred spring or holy well that carries with it protective properties. Failing this, have some ordinary water and add to it three drams of holy water. Place your hands over the water and repeat the Lord's Prayer. Take the rowan sprig and in front of the client start to asperse them head to toe with the water whilst saying:

*Our Lord stood by the rowan tree
and there he decreased the evil from nine until it was
nothing
from 9 to 8
from 8 to 7
from 7 to 6
from 6 to 5
from 5 to 4
from 4 to 3
from 3 to 2
from 2 to 1*

And then 1 to nothing, he stripped the man/woman of the evil eye then they were free and stood by Our Lords right side.

Keep this invocation nine times. At the last word, end the final charm with the sealing words:

FIAT FIAT FIAT!

With the remaining water, cross the head of the patient, both hands and feet, as well as the side of the ribs representing the 5 wounds of Christ. (nobody knows truly what side of the ribs Christ's final wound was, any side will suffice.)

A new Charm against House Fires

According to the grimoire Albertus Magnus Egyptian secrets, which gave a lot of influence to the cousin of British cunning craft practice of folk magic known as Pennsylvanian Pow Wow, in order for a person to stop fires, a person is to take a plate inscribing upon it the famous SATOR Square, it is then thrown into the fire. This is said to stop the fire in its tracks, a modern idea would be to beautifully inscribe the charm upon a plate and hang it in the threshold of the homestead to ward against house fires.

SATOR
AREPO
TENET
OPERA
ROTAS

Against Sorcery

On a Good Friday, take Elmwood and cut out chips from this wood 1-2 inches in length. Cut them out whilst calling the three holiest names: The father, the son, and the holy spirit. Carve three crosses into them and wherever such a slip is placed, all sorcery will be banished.

-Egyptian secrets Albertus magnus.

To stop witches looking into your house through supernatural means

In Essex, known also in older times as witch country, it was said to stop witches seeing into your business, hang up bunches of the plant St John's Wort in the windows. This will prevent them from seeing in and spying on you through any supernatural means.

-Essex: its forest, folk and folklore J. H Clarke & co.

Another interesting mention of St john's wort in witchcraft prevented, mentions hanging the plant in your house hinders mischievous acts and puts to flight evil spirits. Another charm similar found in this book calls upon hanging Mugwort by your front door to preserve the house from witchcraft.

To Stop Nightmares and being Hagridden

Place a pair of your shoes at the end of your bed facing away from you. This will stop nightmares as the shoes facing away will ward away any evil spirits that want to plague you with bad dreams. It will also stop being hag ridden or what's now known as sleep Paralysis which is seen as the brain waking up before the body. It was believed that a hag had sat on the chest of the victim and plagued them. I have a friend where this would occur a for a while, but then I told him to go and sprinkle flaxseeds on the side of his table by his bed and it stopped. The idea that the hag felt compelled to count every seed before attempting to hag ride her victim. By the time she had finished counting, the sun would rise, and she would disperse away. This idea of spirits having to count individual small items is prevalent within British folk magic and lore.

For example, within the northwest of England, there is a spirit known as The Boggart which is a mischievous and malevolent spirit that would do harm to those around the house or to landscapes it was tied to. It did in a lot of cases have links to the benevolent brownie believing the brownie had become offended in some way by having offerings of clothing given to it by those of the household or that its work it supplied the house had been taken fun of or criticised. A handful of flaxseeds would be thrown around the threshold that he terrorised thus, keeping him busy from causing any carnage or mischief until all the seeds were individually counted. To further add to this, a handful of salt would be placed in the rooms the activity was occurring as it was believed spirits of the land cannot abhor salt in any way, along with an iron horseshoe nailed to the door to ward away the boggart, however unfortunately in a lot of cases trying to get rid of the boggart wasn't always successful. In Yorkshire, a farmer named George Cheetham and his family attempted to flee their own house from a boggart that had taken residence in its home and was causing misery and misfortune to the whole household. As the neighbour asked them if they were leaving the boggarts voice spoke out in front of the farmer and his family to the neighbour: *"Aye were fleeing!"* once the family heard this they turned straight around as they knew the spirit would follow them wherever they went.

The Abracadabra Charm

Taken from *Nummits and crummits* by Sarah Hewett, the following charm is used to ward away witchcraft, pixies, and spirits and the forces of evil. An interesting point is that it's the only historical reference so far that I personally have seen to the term 'grey witch.'

It reads as such: *The word 'Abracadabra' written on parchment was given by an Exeter white witch, to perform who desired to possess a talisman against the dominion of the grey witch, pixies, evil spirit's and the powers of darkness. It cost a guinea, and sewn up in a small black silk bag one inch square. This was hung round the neck and never removed. Should it by chance fall to the ground, all its properties for good would be lost and a new charm must be procured from the same white witch, or dire misfortune would overtake the owner.*

A sure test to discover if a child is influenced under the evil eye

A sure way to tell whether or not a child has been fascinated or overlooked, is to gather 3 oak apples and drop them in a basin of water underneath the child's cradle whilst observing the strictest silence. If they sink, the child is affected and has been overlooked. If they swim the child is free from any malefic influence.

Consult the Oracle

Charms against the evil eye in children

There are many ways to deter the evil eye. Firstly, is sweeping a child's face with a bough of pine; laying a piece of turf cut from a young boys grave and placing it under the pillow of the bewitched boy, as the same is done for girls. Hanging up the keys to the house over the child's cradle, or hanging round its neck fennel seeds, or Hawthorn also known as 'Bread and Cheese' as children would eat the younger leaves of these plants. If we look at Hawthorn, it does have conflicting folklore here as it is said to never be brought into the house only during mayday as it will upset the Faerie folk.

Consult the Oracle

Sator Mirror

If you feel you have had the evil eye put upon your home and hearth and wish to send it back, Cecil Williamson recommended as a way to turn back curses and ill wishes from your home and back to the sender. A mirror with the reflective side was fixed behind the front door facing outwards to counteract and send back any maleficia sent towards the home and hearth. An alteration of this, would be to inscribe clearly in black ink at the back of the mirror the famous SATOR square thus invoking and calling more protective powers:

SATOR
AREPO
TENET
OPERA
ROTAS

To Frustrate the powers of the Black Witch

Take a cast iron horseshoe and nail it over the door pointing up. Whilst nailing it up chant in a monotone manner the following incantation:

So as the fire do melt the wax,
And wind blows smoke away,
So in the presence of the Lord
The wicked shall decay, the wicked shall decay.

-Sarah Hewett Nummits and Crummits.

To be utterly rid of the witch and hang her up by her hair

This intriguing charm is mentioned in reginald scots discoverie of witchcraft. Unfortunately, one of the issues is with this charm is that it does not supply the characters mentioned in the book. I will still supply this as this could create inspiration for those who may wish to modify this charm to their own suiting and needs, an idea could be a seal of saturn.

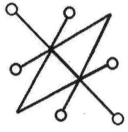

You must obtain some earth from a dead man's grave, forming an image of the witch and baptising it in their name. where on this image, the witches name must be written with a unknown character inscribed into this also. Then the image must be perfumed with rotten bone and then the following psalms read backwards:

Domine dominus noster, dominus illuminatio mea, Domine exaudi orationem meam, deus laudem meam ne tacueris.

It is to be buried first in one place then in another. This is said to destroy the witch. (Pictured: Saturn seal)

An Isle of Mann charm using right footprint dirt to rid someone of the evil eye.

If a person" said train, *"wishes to purchase an animal, but will not give the price demanded, the disposer lifts earth from the print made by the person's right foot on the ground, where he stood to drive the bargain, and rubs the animal with it, to prevent the effects of what is called by*

142

the islanders overlooking." This account is taken from Folklore of the isle of Mann written by A. W Moore in 1891. This charm is used to counteract any bewitchments or overlooking when selling cattle. It involves one very simple method, gathering the dust from the right foot of where the suspected witch who sent the evil eye has stood, and then disperse the dust over the person or animal affected. There seem to be in witch lore, a lot of accounts, tales and ballads of the evil eye being used on cattle in general. This same charm wasn't just bound to the selling of cattle for that matter, the first story mentions a ploughman who witnessed a hare cross over afield and stare at a team of his horses. His horses then become lame and were said to instantly drop dead after the creatures sighting. The ploughman remembering older lore, took some of the dirt where the hare was stood, and sprinkled it over the horses and they had sprung back to life as if nothing had happened.

Another similar tale, speaks of a man who lived on the south side of The Isle of Mann who had a calf that had suddenly fallen ill. He then saw an old woman crossing a path and decided to gather dirt from her right footprint, sprinkling it over the calf who was said to rapidly recover.

When the possessor of the evil eye was discovered, the next step was to cure the disease, and this was frequently effected by picking up the dust from beneath the feet or from the threshold of the suspected witch and rubbing it on her victim.

As mentioned earlier, we can see that most of the time cattle charming can also be worked upon humans too and so many cattle charming spells can be interchangeable. Why the right foot? It's not entirely clear, but a part of me cannot help but think that gathering from the right rather than the left is to represent the side that was seen as benevolence. Whereas the left at a certain time in history was said to represent the more sinistral aspect of life ie: the left-hand path.

To find out a thief

Touch the suspected thief with the herb vervain, and the guilty person shall cry.

-The grimoire of Arthur Gauntlet

Thwarting the Evil Eye

Taken from the Carmina Gadelica, this spell makes the use of a running stream which is mentioned as a place where the living and the dead pass, as well as a wooden ladle and metal. According also to this charm, the person removing the evil eye must also be of the opposite sex to the afflicted. The ladle also cannot in any instances be made of metal, it must be made entirely of wood according to this charm. Another rule is that the metal according to alexander Carmichael has to be copper or gold if the patient is male or silver and brass if the patient is female. The magician goes to a nearby running stream, takes the ladle and lifts up the water in the name of the three highest names: *The Father, the son, and the holy spirit.*

They then place a piece of gold brass, silver, or copper in the ladle, whilst the sign of the holy cross is made over the water and the following rhyme is spoken in a slow, recitative manner over the water with the name of the patient at the end of the charm:

Who shall thwart the evil eye?
I shall thwart it, methinks,
In name of the King of life.
Three seven commands so potent,
Spake Christ in the door of the city;

Pater Mary one,
Pater King two,
Pater Mary three,
Pater King four,
Pater Mary five,
Pater King six,
Pater Mary seven;
Seven pater Maries will thwart
The evil eye,
Whether it be on man or on beast,
On horse or on cow;
Be thou in thy full health this night,

[The name]
In name of the Father, the Son, and the Holy Spirit.

Amen.

There is also a Gàidhlig version of the prayer. For the sake of preserving Scots Gàidhlig as a language, and the history of this charm, I feel it is only right to provide the Gàidhlig version to credit the charm in its entirety:

Co a thilleas cronachduinn suil?
Tillidh mise tha mi 'n duil,
Ann an ainm Righ nan dul.

Tri seachd gairmeachdain co ceart,
Labhair Criosd an dorusd na cathrach;
    Paidir Moire a h-aon,
    Paidir Righ a dha,
    Paidir Moire a tri,
    Paidir Righ a ceithir,
    Paidir Moire a coig,
    Paidir Righ a sia,
    Paidir Moire a seachd;
Tillidh seachd paidrichean Moire
Cronachduinn suil,
Co dhiubh bhitheas e air duine no air bruid,
Air mart no air earc;
Thusa bhi na d' h-ioma shlainte nochd,
    [An t-ainm]
An ainm an Athar, a Mhic, 's an Spioraid Naoimh.

    Amen.

    The water is then given to the patient to drink, or it can be aspersed upon the patient's head and back bone. In the case of cattle, a thread with the same colour of the animal charmed is tied around the cattle's tail, and if the animal has horns, they must be anointed with the water after the aspersing. The remaining water must not be spilled and is to be poured upon a stone or a rock in which it was said that if the sickness be severe would split the stone.

<u>A Quick Cleansing ritual</u>

For this contemporary working, gather some Holy water from a church, anointing it on the top of your back/shoulders so that you're washing away any influences sent by a suspected evil doer. Then asperse the water to your hands, so that your hands are cleansed from being entwined and entangled in any curses. Lastly, wash your feet in the remaining water so you're no longer walking into anything that has been worked against your favour.

To Beat Witches

Let the sweepings, which are swept together in a house for three days remain in a heap and on the third day, cover it with a black cloth made of drilling. Then take a stick of an elm tree and flog the dirt heap bravely, and the sorceress must assist, or you will batter her to death. Probatum (tested in latin.) taken from Egyptian secrets.

To burn a Witch so that she receives pock marks over her entire body

Take butter from the household larder, render it down in an iron pot until it broils then take ivy or wintergreen and fry it; take three nails of a coffin and stick them in the sauce; carry the mass to a place where neither sun nor moon shines into, and the witch will be sick for half a year. Taken from Egyptian secrets.

The Devils Cookbook:
Curses and Maledictions

Image: Transcendental magic its doctrine and ritual Eliphas Levi

Cursing well

Holy wells throughout the ages have been used for healing and charming alike, there are sacred and holy wells that have gained reputations for their use in a more sinister manner. A famous example of cursing in this way, comes from the ancient roman idea of inscribing a lead cursing tablet and disposing it in the spring dedicated to the goddess sious minerva found in the roman springs in bath. Taken from the welsh fairy book by W. Jenkyn Thoma in 1908, Goronwy Tudor and the Witches of Llanddona, is a curious tale describing a man's encounter with the famous witches of Llanddona. Not only does it give an example of cursing magic within wells, but it also gives some good methods for counter acting damage done by malicious conjuring against a person:

Goronwy Tudor and the Witches of Llanddona

Very few men in Anglesey in the olden days dared to cross any of the Witches of Llanddona, and those who were bold enough to do so suffered grievously for their rashness. But Goronwy Tudor, who lived not far from Llanddona, was reckless enough to defy even Bella Fawr, Big Bella, the most famous and most dreaded of all the witches of that uncanny village, and he was not a ha'porth the worse. Perhaps you do not know the history of the Llanddona witches. Long ago a boat came ashore in Red Wharf Bay without rudder or oars, full of men and women half dead with hunger and thirst. In early days it was the custom to put evil-doers in a boat to drift oarless and rudderless on the sea, and when this boat- was swept by wind and waves on the beautiful sands of Llanddona, the good people who then lived there prepared to drive it back into the sea, thinking it was manned by criminals. But the strangers caused a spring of pure water to burst forth on the sands (the well still remains), and this decided their fate. They were allowed to stay and to build cottages. But they did not change their evil natures. The men lived by smuggling, and the women begged and practised witchcraft. It was impossible to overcome the smugglers in a fray, for each of them carried about with him a black fly tied in a knot of his neckerchief. When their strength failed them in the fight they undid the knots of their cravats, and the flies flew at the eyes of their opponents and blinded them. The women used to visit the farmhouses, and when they asked for a pound of butter, a loaf of bread, some potatoes, eggs, a fowl, part of a pig, or what not, they were not denied, because they cursed those who refused them. If they attended a fair or market, no one ventured to bid against them for anything.

But Goronwy Tudor was not afraid of them. He had a birthmark above his breast, which is a great protection against witchcraft, and he knew how to break nearly every spell. He had the plant which is called Mary's turnip growing in front of his house: he also nailed horseshoes above every door, and put rings made of the mountain ash under the doorposts, thus making his house and all his farm buildings safe. To make them doubly sure he sprinkled earth from the churchyard in all his rooms, and in his byre, stable and pigstye. When the animals were in the fields, however, he had some difficulty in securing them from harm. One day when he went to fetch his cows from the meadow to be milked he found them sitting like cats before a fire, with their hind legs beneath them. Goronwy took the skin of an adder, burnt it and scattered the ashes over the horns of the cows. They got up at once, and walked off with their usual dignity to the byre. Another day the milk would not turn into butter, and a very unpleasant smell arose from the churn. Goronwy took a crowbar, heated it red hot, and put it in the milk. Out jumped a large hare, and ran away through the open door of the dairy. After this the milk was churned into beautiful butter. Some time after the supply of milk began to decline, and the butter made from it was so bad and evil-smelling that the very dogs would not touch it. The milk became scantier and scantier, until at last it ceased altogether, and the cows gave nothing but blood. Goronwy watched in the fields at night and saw a hare going up to a cow and sucking it. She squirted from her mouth and nostrils the milk she had sucked, and then went on to another cow. She did the same with her and with all the other cows. Goronwy knew that it was old Bella in the form of a hare, and he prepared to stop her evildoing and to punish her. The next night he took his gun, putting into it a silver coin instead of shot (shot cannot penetrate a witch's body), and placed a bit of vervain under the stock. When he saw the hare milking the cows he fired at her. The hare immediately ran off in the direction of Bella's cottage, with Goronwy after her. He was not so fleet of foot as puss, but he managed to keep her in sight, and saw her jumping over the lower half of the door of the house. Going up to the cottage he heard the sound of dreadful groans. When he reached the door he went in. There was no hare to be seen, but old Bella was sitting by the fire with blood streaming from her legs. He was never again troubled by old Bella in the shape of a hare, and by drawing blood from the bewitched kine he broke the spell.

Bella made one more attempt to injure him. She went to the Cold Well and launched at him the great curse of the Witches of Llanddona:

> *May he wander for ages many,*
> *And at every step, a stile,*
> *At every stile, a fall;*
> *At every fall, a broken bone,*
> *Not the largest nor the least bone,*
> *But the chief neckbone, every time.*

Goronwy felt in his bones that he had been cursed. He got some witch's butter that grows on decayed trees and stuck pins in it. When the pain inflicted by the pins penetrated her body, Bella had willy-nilly to appear before him. She was screaming with pain, and Goronwy refused to take the pins which were causing the anguish out of the butter until she said: *"Rhad Duw ac ar bopeth ar a feddi—God's blessing on thee and on everything that thou possessest."* After this neither Bella nor any of her tribe had any power over Goronwy or his wife, or his man-servant or his maid-servant, or his ox or his ass, or anything that was his."

To lay spirits by an anathema

Ye persons look upon me for a moment till I draw three blood drops from you, which ye have fortified. The first I draw from yor teeth, the other from your lung, the third I draw from your hearts own main; with this I take your hosts away and ye shall stand till I remove from ye the iron band.

Three times spoken taken from Egyptian secrets

The rite of transference

Mentioned in rowan tree and red thread, this charm will transfer the illness of one to another. According to the story, Allie Nisbet was said to take a pail of boiling water and bathing the patients' legs in it; she dipped her fingers into the vessel and ran widdershins (anticlockwise) around the persons sick bed three times saying:

The bones to the fire and the soul to the devil.

By doing this, she had transferred the illness to another woman who had later died less than 24 hours after the conjuration had been complete.

Betty Trenoweth's Curse

A curse in the book 'An Joan the crone' and Robert hunts book popular romances of the west of England, gives an account of a quarrel that started between two women known as Betty Trenoweth and Mary Noy. The quarrel all started with eggs, then a throw of stones, then escalated into this full-blown malediction we see before us:

>*Mary Noy thou ugly, old and spiteful plague,*
>*I give thee the collick, the palsy and ague.*
>*All the eggs thy fowl lay, from this shall be addle,*
>*All thy hens have the pip and die with the straddle.*
>*And before nine moons have come and gone,*
>*If all they copies (chickens) there shan't live one;*
>*Thy arm and thy hand, that cast the stone*
>*Shall wither and waste skin to bone.*

Or a more colourful malediction is also contained In Robert hunts book popular romances of the west of England 1903:

>*Madam Noy, you ugly old bitch,*
>*You shall have the gout, the palsy, and itch;*
>*All the eggs your hens lay henceforth shall be addle;*
>*All your hens have the pip, and die with the straddle;*
>*And ere I with the mighty fine madam have done, Of her*
>*favourite 'coppice' she shan't possess one.*

The Hereford Curse Doll

Found in 1870 in Hereford, was an interesting artefact which held within it an absolute brutal, yet intriguing curse attached to it directed toward a Mary Ann Ward. The effigy was a rustic and crudely made doll, out of wood and its arms and legs made from cotton material with fabric attached to it, containing a written curse which was inputted into the fold of its dress. The image was secreted in the crevice of the brickwork in the house of number 21 in East Street. The charm read the following:

Mary Ann, I act this spell upon you from my whole heart, wishing you to never rest nor eat nor sleep the rester part of your life. I hope your flesh will waste away and I hope you will never spend another penny I ought to have. Wishing this from my whole heart.

This could be recreated and hid in somebody's threshold like the original charm mentioned above, or even by their threshold so that just like the witch bottle, the charm has frequent contact with the victim. Thus, delivering the wasting effect upon the victim themselves.

To make a person dance

There really is no other way telling this story that's not going to make me look delusional. For the sake of what happened, and it being relevant to the modern world, I think it's only fair I include this charm. If we look in different books of magic, particularly within the tradition of grimoires, we can see that there seems to be spells to make a woman dance. Such a conjuration is found in a myriad of grimoires, utilising different techniques in order to achieve this. A while back at a wedding, I was with a good friend of mine and we came across what would be known as one of the most horrible, and obnoxious people I have ever met in my life. From the get-go she proceeded to slate somebody down for how their body looked and actively was trying to get others to participate in her body shaming exercises. The day carried on and the woman continued upsetting others at this wedding, at times really overstepping the mark. The line was crossed when she greatly upset a friend's sibling on her wedding day.

    Myself and my friend, took a serviette and a pen, then proceeding to draw out an 8-pointed wheel similar to the design from Reginald Scots discoverie of witchcraft to control spirits as that was our main inspiration. Onto each point we included different aspects of her, so for instance she had very curly hair and we drew curly hair onto the image, she had high heels and so they came onto the image. Each point held something that represented herself and what we associated with her. After this was done, we held the image in our hands staring with intent towards her directing our intentions. The image or sigil for that matter, was placed onto the floor, and with our feet we tapped along to the melody of the song played. Well, lo and behold she started dancing but dancing in such a way that was so forced and people started staring at her in the strangest way as she was acting completely different. It was honestly the most comical thing ive seen in my life, people around her were pointing and laughing, whilst myself and my friend were in absolute stitches jiving our legs on top of the sigil.

This started with one song and five songs down the line she was still dancing even though people were actively trying to get her to sit down. I couldn't belive it, it was without a doubt one of the funniest moments in my life and il honestly never hear the song footloose the same way again!

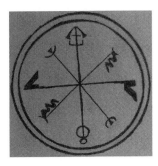

The image presented by the title, is taken from Reginald Scots Discoverie of witchcraft. Whilst the image on the presented here, is a crude sketch by me, of the symbolisms she had. (2 shoes, handbag, diamond ring, curly hair)

'*Picture aft she makes of ony ane she hates- and gars expire with slaw and racking pins afore the fire stuck fu' of pins, the devlish picture melt; the pain by folk they represent is met.*

-Rowan tree and red thread

With Binding of Thorns

The following charm is something I came up with myself, it is worked to bind those who have hurtful intentions towards you, this conjuration works in a way that will make sure their harmful words and actions come back upon them rather than you. It is something that I have worked over the years, and I wanted to share it with you as it has brought much success in the past. The idea is to create an 'image' or a doll representing the troublemaker, adding into it any personal effects of the person which can range from; hair, nails, pubic hair, spit, urine, semen/sexual fluids. Create this doll out of a dish cloth and wool/twine making sure it is biodegradable. Form the images Head, making sure to add into it the personal effects of the person intended. Then once the head is made form the arms, body, and legs of the effigy. Then can begin the baptism, take this by a running river immersing the image into the water stating:

"I baptise thee in the name of (full name of target) by water creature of cloth I name thee (name) thou art (name)."

Take the effigy out of the water and from that point, taking the doll in your hands. Breathe life into the images mouth, seeing it as now linked to your intended target. Be sure to get some decent gardening gloves for this working and some biodegradable twine, as the next step involves you wrapping brambles around the effigy making sure they're completely strangulating the doll of said victim. Tie this with twine so that as the bramble grows, so shall the persons actions forever turn on them as they will be bound by their own hurtful actions.

The Witches Ladder

I'd like to say that the witch's ladder has a historical tie to folk witchcraft, but as you will see reading on this isn't entirely the truth. A witches ladder is an object used within folk magic for Inflicting harm upon somebody or people, but it can be used for several different purposes other than the art of tudding. The intentions are normally 'knotted in' thus representing the witches will being tied into the charm representing a malediction or another intention towards a targeted person. The charm was said to typically be left around the persons threshold to work its intent into them. The first account of the device known as 'the witch's ladder' was the wellington witches' ladder that was found in Wellington somerset in an old house which was demolished in 1878. The room was found inaccessible from the inside of the house which contained an armchair and 6 brooms as well as the famous ladder in question. The brooms had become withered and the feathers on the ladder were aged so much that some had fallen away. There was a lot of speculation as to what the original purpose of this actually was. Many theories coming from famous folklorists such as Charles Godfrey Leyland, who drew comparison to an object known as the witches garland used by Italian witches. Which was said to again contain maledictions, made of wool and black hen feathers which he said would be plucked whilst the poor creatures were alive. The charm Was said to also hold an image of a hen or cock barring a cross of black pins and then to be placed under the victims bed working its ill intent towards the target. As well as folklorists, reverends such as Sabine Baring Gould who said the ladder was made of black wool alongside white or brown thread whilst a cockerel's feather, was inputted into it every two inches with it the witch weaving in maledictions and ailments they wanted the victim to experience. According to the reverend, to release the ladders grip on person, It would then be thrown into the bottom of Dozmary pond in bodmin moor where it was believed as the bubbles rose from the charm, so the malediction was released, thus releasing the victim of the tudding or the curse. They were then instructed to go to church whilst a baptism is being carried out where a spell was recited and the person then was bathed in holy water to remove them of the malediction. The link between water and the witch's ladder is interesting, as Leyland said the way to rid yourself of this curse would be to throw the garland into a running river, which once again re-iterates the idea that running water has the ability to kill or wash away the Hex or charm cast against you.

However, the reality is here with the witch's ladder, that we only have what we have found throughout history. No one really can say for definite what the witches' ladder was designed for or even if it is even historically witchcraft. It has however become adopted in folk witchcraft and folk magic in general being used for a myriad of different purposes and I can say from personal experience it works! I have utilised this charm for many different purposes other than its malefic reputation it has gained; I've actually used this in the ways to find employment and it worked very well. To start off with, I firstly before anything called my familiar spirits and asked them to assist and help me during this working. I took an orange cord symbolising power and success and took three small in thickness but longer in length threads of the cord and tied them altogether. From there I started to plait them into a cord, and with that plaiting into it my will and intention. The whole time I kept my focus as strong as I could focusing only on the intent and desired outcome. I was speaking out this intention again and again whilst this cord was bound and was tied at the end with a piece of free cord to seal it and stop it becoming unwound. After that, I made nine small knots in it and with each knot I held the knot up before it was being tied, speaking my intention into it directly then knotting the cord with force. I done this nine times, making sure this time to not knot into it any feathers as I made it to wear along my right wrist, so its influence would forever been in my presence, working away its intent. After the ladder had been made, I then took some water that had come from a sacred well (I realise people may not have sacred wells or springs around the corner so if not, some Holy water will suffice.) I baptised to what my intentions were, a good statement for this could be:

Hear my words and hear them now, you are made for the sole purpose of getting me a job, and you will provide me with such, a job will come my way one which will serve me well financially and keep me financially stable. For this purpose, I baptise you.

      The ladder was then placed around my right wrist and the idea was I wore it till it fell off or until I found a job. Within days after looking, I had managed to secure a job and there was something extremely powerful about weaving into something your will and intention, whilst stating clearly what you want, it's something that can be done so simplistically yet so effectively. Another thing to consider here, is what feathers may have what significance to what virtues and powers it is you desire in your working. If you're not lucky to find some or in a rush, then I have admittedly in the past used feathers from a craft store. White can be used for benevolent purposes, whilst black can be used for malevolent purposes. However, if you have time do go outside and forage for your own and please I'm sure you won't, but for the love of God make sure you forage them ethically as they are found. Perhaps by asking the spirits for feathers that will be contributary to your working whilst giving an offering in exchange could be a good idea? I'd hate the thought of somebody inflicting pain on some poor defenceless animal for their feathers. I must add, these are my own thoughts on these feathers and what they represent to me through my study of folklore and stories they are NOT set in stone so please don't see this as the traditional meanings for feathers and their symbolism:

Black hen and black cockerel feathers: mentioned as above.

Swan feathers- used for marriage and love, swans are powerfully known for their romantic pairings and their influences. With their association also with St Brigid through the discovery of Saveok witch pits, they can also be used for fertility and pregnancy spells.

Love bird feathers- not surprisingly, used for Love and romance once again, these birds sit in pairs and although not native to the UK, they have been brought over domestically as pets.

Dove feathers: used to bring peace to people who suffer with anxiety/depression/helping them through bad situations, also hung up in the kitchen the centre of the home for a manic household to ensure that it grants peace to all those within it. Can also be used to establish higher power connections and healing as it carries the representation of the holy spirit and because of that, can also be used for spiritual protection against harm.

Magpie feathers: The magpie is the king of thieves, he is an absolute sucker for shiny objects and so it is no surprise that their feathers are used to ward away thieves acting as a deterrent against them. A good point is to make sure to place this ladder high up in the threshold so that it will be the only highest thief in the threshold.

This is done so that any other thief would be lower and not allowed into the threshold where the charm resides.

The magpie's feathers can also be used in conjunction with the old superstitious rhyme: One for sorrow, two for joy, three for a girl and four for a boy, five for silver, six for gold, seven for a secret never to be told.

The number of feathers can be put upon a ladder to bring these influences, so for instance a singular magpie feather suspended onto a ladder along with 8 black feathers tied alongside it would be used to bring sorrow to somebody.

Or in a more positive light, two magpie feathers alongside 7 white feathers may be used to bring joy. The magpie has a fearsome reputation associated with the faery folk and their realm, so if you're conducting a working involving them then this is a great choice but please be careful.

Pidgeon feathers: Years ago (and I'm talking years) long before the invention of Mobile phones, people would use the pigeon as a carrier so that it would be able to deliver messages to others and let them know of any information.

Its obvious powers it bestows, is of communication and sending messages, perhaps you're needing somebody to call you? Messages to the other side can also be worked into the ladder along with the feather of the pigeon to get a message over. (If you want to get the message over quick, then the day of Wednesday which mercury rules over will work really well for this.)

Crow Feathers: the feathers of the crow could again be used for the above as the crow is often seen as a messenger to the spirit world. In saying this, it can be used in much more sinister and destructive charms to send disastrous harm onto somebody. The crow is also the bird of death so its feathers can also be used to put death to a situation.

Woodpecker feathers: Used for chipping away boundaries or barriers you have in front of you. Need a promotion? Keep having the same problem occur? Need to move forward? Woodpecker feathers are great for making sure your boundaries are chipped away and that no task is too difficult. I would in no way say this is a road opening like in the Hoodoo tradition, because this is not hoodoo its another folk magical tradition, but it would be the nearest comparison to that.

Owl feathers: Associated with the night and the supernatural, the owl is seen as a bird that is able to hex or curse bringing dismay and bad luck upon any person. In the west country, they use the term owl blinking for cursing or placing a hex upon somebody.

Cuckoo Feathers: If you're lucky enough to find these feathers, these are great for being able to disguise yourself when casting against other magical practitioners. The reason behind this is the cuckoo is the master of illusion staying in another's nest convincing the other birds it is their offspring when it's not, acting as a parasite. This can also be used to have control or influence over others.

Goose feather: This can be used to add finance or money into a situation, as it is associated with having your belly full from the term fat as a goose. Also, it is said than on Michael mass day if you eat goose, you will not want or need for money the whole year following.

Canadian Goose feathers: You know for Canadians, they're not that friendly?! Canadian geese are fiercely protective, they will stop at no means if they feel threatened and are able to do a lot of damage. They have tremendous wing strength on them and have a terrifying hiss. Because of this reason and for that alone, they are used as a fierce protection against negative people in your life.

Feathers from caged birds: These can be used to influence somebody or to manipulate them into doing your will.

Duck feathers: Used to keep yourself afloat in hard times, and to be able to overcome any situation no matter what the tides bring. Also used for any water spirits influences.

Hen feathers: used for healing and fertility, great to use at times of health troubles particularly with ill health in children because hens nurture chicks.

How to curse somebody using the ladder

I am now going to give you an example of cursing somebody using the witches ladder, as I'd feel bad not giving the instructions for using it for malefic purposes as it has gained a sinister reputation first and foremost. Once again before the operation begins, call in your spirit helpers/familiars asking for their help and assistance in your working. Then obtain some of the persons personal effects as well as three equal lengths of twine, braiding these into a plaited cord. The whole time doing this use your imagination and visualising what you want to happen to the victim. As this is being done, you can call out their full name with anger, repeating it over and over again.

Visualise them being hexed and overlooked by your influences and allow this repetition to take you into a light trance. After this has been done, take the weaved twine and then call out the following:

(Name of person) (Name of person) (Name of person)

Nine/Thirteen times I call you out, by this cord and by your threads of fate,

In the Devils name I call you forth and inflict this harm upon you,

wishing it from my whole heart, inflicting pain and misery into your life.

I wrangle your threads of fate and fray them,

I twist and turn your life

And set about your suffering!

Call this out nine or thirteen times. After this has been done, take your cord and knot 9 to 13 knots in the cord and within each knot, tie in their hair along with a black feather of your choosing. Speak out the person's name with the statement you want to happen to them, you could do nine or thirteen misfortunes but generally I find keeping things singular for me has more of an impact. So, for instance:

I curse you (name of person) may your life turn to shit.

Tie each knot aggressively making sure the feather and hair is firmly in the ladder, until this is complete. Take the ladder to a person's whereabouts, where they are able to pass through it each time that they're picking up the intent and energies from the ladder. It could be secreted by their household, their workplace, hidden in things such as hidden into a person's mattress, hidden in a tree nearby their house, make sure it's hard to find because if it is found its easier for somebody to backfire those intentions and maledictions that onto you if they're skilled in the magical arts.

If you're using sexual fluids and urine and the person happens to be a man, these could be smeared onto the cord once its braided and could then be used for  rendering him impotent as the string can be a good representation of the phallus. In terms of feathers for impotency, Crow feathers would be good use as they would put death to his penis making him impotent, his pants could also be knotted in with crows feathers instead of fluids. These again are just an idea of how one would utilise the darker aspects of the ladder. Pictured below: a ladder made by myself.

Conjuring wind and storms

A wizard known in the Scottish Highlands as 'Macpherson of power' (Mac-Mhuirich nam buadh in scots Gaidhlig) was travelling by sea on a calm day and the skipper had asked him if he was able to raise wind, he insisted this was something he was able to do and repeated the following invocation:

> *An east wind from the calm aether,*
>
> *As the Lord of the elements has ordained,*
>
> *A wind that needs not rowing nor reefing,*
>
> *That will do nought deceitful to us.*

At this point the skipper had told him this was a weak wind he had summoned and so Macpherson had then proceeded to say:

> *a north wind hard as a rod,*
>
> *Struggling again like a gunwale,*
>
> *Like a red roe sore pressed,*
>
> *Descending a hillocks narrow hard head*

Once again the skipper protested telling the wizard how this doesn't do his abilities justice and so with that the wizard proceeded to perform the following conjuration:

> *If there be a wind in cold hell,*
>
> *Devil: send it after us,*
>
> *In waves and surges.*
>
> *And if one goes ashore let it be I,*
>
> *And if two, I and my dog.*

A terrible sea came and rolled the entirety of the ship over that drowned everybody, apart from Mac-Vuirich and his dog who were the only ones to survive.

-witchcraft and second sight in the highlands and islands of Scotland.

To stop Nosey people from looking in

These days, with the rise of social media people really do want to know what other people are doing a lot more. Humans are inquisitive beings by nature but sometimes people really do need to "mind their own" where it doesn't concern them. The following spell given is a way which it will stop 'prying eyes' into your life where it doesn't concern them. Take an eye of an animal (a fisheye works brilliant, as it's a fantastic way to truly use up all the parts of the animal when buying it for a meal.) Take a sharp long needle and pierce the eye stating the person's name out loud three times. Then take the plant from the nettle family known as: Soleirolia Soleirolii what's also knowns as mind your own business, wrapping it around the impaled eye and burying the impaled eye in your back garden to make folks mind their own business. If you don't have a back garden a pot of earth on your balcony will do or place a pot of earth in the furthest away part of the vicinity. Another charm is to carry the plant mind your own business around with you if you don't want nosey or prying eyes upon you generally, especially when you are venturing out into the woods to practice!

To lame a horse

I want to add before this spell, this is not something that I actively encourage, it is merely here for historical value. Go to a churchyard and take a nail from a coffin that has served its time in the grave, and when you see a horse that you wish to be lamed. Go to where the horse has passed and stab the nail into the print-mark of his foot, and it will take the same effect as if stabbed the same distance in the frog of the foot, and he immediately becomes lame.

-an exposition on the miller and horseman's word or the true system of raising the devil

To compel a Dog, Horse, or any other animal to follow you

Caspar guide thee, Balthasar bind thee, Melchoir keep thee.

This is to be uttered three times into the right ear.

Take from Egyptian secrets.

Miscellaneous/ all-purpose conjurations

Of Fascination or Binding by Sight

Fascination is the art of binding somebody by sight and eye contact carried from one person to another. With this ability, any intentions can be accomplished, either by means of drawing somebody in for love, or by overlooking them with ill intent. This Excerpt is taken from Francis Barrett's book the Magus which was published in 1801 and took a lot of influences from other grimoires the most prominent being the four books of occult philosophy from Cornelius Agrippa, this book was not only also used by cunning folk and the realms of folk magic but as mentioned, became one the building blocks of the western magical traditions altogether.

We call fascination a binding, because it is effected by a look, glance, or observation in which we take a possession of the spirit, and overpower the same, of those we mean to fascinate or suspend; for it comes through the eyes, and the instrument by which we fascinate or bind is a certain, pure, lucid, subtill spirit, generated out of the ferment of the purer blood by the heart of the heart, and the firm, determined, and ardent will of the soul which directs it to the object previously disposed to be fascinated. This doth always send forth by the eye's rays or beams, carrying with them a pure subtill spirit or vapour into the eye or blood of him or her that is opposite. So, the eye, being opened and intent upon anyone with a strong imagination, doth dart its beams, which are the vehicle of the spirit, into whatever we will affect or bind, which spirit striking the eye of them who are fascinated, being stirred up in the heart and soul of him that sends them forth, and possessing the breath of them who are struck, wounds their hearts, infects their spirits, and overpowers them.

Know likewise, that in witches, those are most bewitched, who, with often looking, direct the edge of their sight to the edge of the sight of those who bewitch or fascinate them; whence arose are the saying of 'Evil Eye' For when the eyes are reciprocally bent one upon the other, and are joined beams to beams, and lights to lights, then the spirits of the one is joined to the spirit of the other, and then are strong ligations made; and most violent love is stirred up, only with a sudden looking on, as it were, with the darting a look, or piercing into the very inmost of the heart, whence the spirit and amorous blood, being thus wounded, are carried forth upon the lover and enchanter; no otherwise than the spirit and the blood of him that is murdered is upon the murderer, who, if standing near the body killed, the blood flows aseth(?), which thing has been tried by repeated experiments.

> *So great power is there in fascination that may uncommon and wonderful things are thereby effected, especially when the vapours of the eyes are subservient to the affection; therefore collieries, ointments, allegations are used to affect and corroborate the spirit in this or that manner: to induce love, they use venereal collyriums, as hippomanes, blood of doves &c. To induce fear, they use martial collyriums, as the eyes of wolves, bears fat, and the civet-cat. To procure misery, or sickness they use saturnine and so on.*

As an added-on idea from this, rather than using animal parts, perhaps having a look at various oils and their astrological and planetary influences. For instance, for Venus, applying very small amounts of an oil around the eyes such as geranium oil, lavender, dragons' blood ect. Perhaps even creating a mix of oils that are pertinent to that ruling planet and influence you wish about to bring and making them within the days of the planets and in the hours of the planets to add to their potency. I will say, from a practical point of view, also being very careful here to make sure no oil gets in the eyes, as well as making sure the oil isn't an irritant in any way to the skin. Rather than applying directly perhaps very small amounts going around the eyes via use of a moisturiser or via use of a base oil. Whenever doing this always pay note to which kind of carrier oil you're using and whether or not they're corrosive to the skin.

In the same chapter of the magus, it speaks of a way to cure being fascinated or bound by sight:

> *"Coral is a well-known preservative against witchcraft and poisons, which if worn now, in this time, as much round children's necks as usual, would enable them to combat many diseases, which their tender years are*

subjected to, and to which, with fascinations, they often fall a victim to. I know how to compose coral amulets, or talismans, which if suspended even by a thread shall (God assisting) prevent all harms and accidents of violence from fire, or water, or witchcraft, and help them to withstand all their diseases."

For Rows and Fights

In the name of God, I do begin, lame your hands and feet because you sin, God grant that I may come out best or never I'll find peace not rest, the true son, master, jesus Christ, died on the cross for all mankind. +++

Egyptian secrets

A charm to open locks

A large part of cunning folk charms and spells that were utilised were the opening of locks. For the point of historical respect, I shall include this spell and also share a funny story. A friend and I were staying at my mother's house, and we were having trouble getting the back door open to let the dog out. We were both a 'tad' intoxicated to say the least and we were trying to open this door over and over again, pushing our drunk selves onto this door giggling, with this my friend looked at me and said: "How many cunning folk does it take to open a lock?!" it was pretty hilarious and I then made a joke about my mum putting a spell on the house saying aloud: "Good god what witchcraft has she put on this?!"

With that the door opened. Which again we found funny. The following charm is taken from witchcraft detected and prevented. I am unfortunately unable to find another term for this herb also. The herbs called Aethiopides will open all locks, with the help of certain words, so be there charms also and periapts, which without any herbs can do as much. Take a piece of wax crossed in baptism, and print certain flowers therein, and tie them in the hinder skirt of your shirt and when you would open the lock, blow thrice there in saying:

Arato hoc portico hoc maratarykin. I open this door in thy name that I am forced to break, as thou breakest hell gets, in nominee patris, and filli and spiritus sancti amen.

Divination by Wax and Water

The following charm was created by myself which I was inspired and based this off the older charms that involve to divine with molten lead and water more formally known as Molybdomancy. The word Molybdos meaning lead and the word nancy meaning to divine. The lead itself is poured through a keyhole. I see no instance of why somebody can't perform this charm pouring the wax through a keyhole too. As this form of divination is using wax, it is technically known as Ceromancy meaning to divine by wax. take a large vessel and fill it high with water, adding a dram of holy water into the vessel. Then take a moment to employ and conjure any familiar spirits you have asking for their assistance and help with your questions. Take a taper candle and light it repeating the Credo prayer:

Credo in Deum Patrem omnipotentem; Creatorem coeli et terrae. Et in Jesum Christum, Filium ejus unicum, Dominum nostrum; qui conceptus est de Spiritu Sancto, natus ex Maria virgine; passus sub Pontio Pilato, crucifixus, mortuus, et sepultus; descendit ad inferna; tertia die resurrexit a mortuis; ascendit ad coelos; sedet ad dexteram Dei Patris omnipotentis; inde venturus (est) judicare vivos et mortuos. Credo in Spiritum Sanctum; sanctam ecclesiam catholicam; sanctorum communionem; remissionem peccatorum; carnis resurrectionem; vitam oeternam.

Amen.

After this has been done then start by dripping the wax into the water, allowing your hands to move around whilst thinking of the question. You can even state it aloud if you so desire. The images that then come out in the wax will indicate the answers given. They may be images of people, or animals/objects. Read into them and see what shapes come out for you and how it corresponds with your question.

Of Botany and Flora

If we look at this earth, we as magicians recognise more so than others how each natural object is imbued with its own spirit or essence and ways in which they can be worked with in order to gain material influence over our desires, such is the ways of animism in its praxis. Many objects over the years have been utilised in folk magic; as you will see throughout this book and the books referenced, that draw upon natural objects for magical means such: as wool, stones, river water, well water, dirt etc. One of the most prominent tools that is used regularly within folk magic is the idea of working with Plants, roots, herbs, and trees. Whether it be drawing the illness from another and passing it onto a tree through the methods of contagion or drawing upon sympathetic elements that a plant may carry, being the properties that are associated with which will fit well within your specific needs of clients you may have, this idea radiates animism and sympathetic magic at its very core. The idea that every natural object has a spirit and that were able to tap into that spirit and work alongside it. Another pointer is if we look regarding the planetary influences each plant may carry and working with their correspondences through that.

In terms of working with plants and plant spirits on a beginning basis, first and foremost I would highly recommend anybody taking on a couple of foraging courses. These are very popular and growing in popularity especially in city areas, these courses allow people to identify certain plants and herbs, as well as give us the opportunity to actually utilise these plants in our food in a safe way that doesn't risk the chance of a misidentification which can lead to poisoning, and in the worst-case scenario death.

Foraging may not necessarily be witchcraft or folk magic per say, but it allows us to grow a further relationship with the natural world around us and gives us that knowledge of our plant allies that unfortunately has become so lost in this day and age. There's nothing better than for myself to go out in springtime and make wild garlic pesto, its healthy, delicious and once again helps form an even tighter link to an actual working relationship with that land. Most practitioners of British folk magic will observe special high days in the yearly calendar which tends to run in line with the agricultural calendars. It's all well and good for us to celebrate these days, but it makes more sense from a practical point of view to be able to physically work in the land were also practicing in, so we are really able to contemplate the seasons and foraging does this.

I am including here a further section of Wort cunning that involves working and utilising plants for occult purposes. I will as always, give the references here for each remedy given, as a disclaimer I will say however, that a person needs to be very careful when ingesting plants/herbs as they may react differently with each person in terms of allergies, conditions, or existing prescriptions/medication. I am not a medical professional, trained botanist, certified herbalist, and do not pretend to be so. In which case I only feel its right to mention this to avoid anyone partaking any injuries and to establish more clarity. I would highly recommend anybody to not ingest plants or herbs that they have no knowledge about themselves. Sadly, within this day and age we tend to be able to identify things like corporate brands more so rather than trees and plants which I believe is another of many examples of our disconnection from nature and the natural world around us. We now rely solely as a species on medicine and pharmaceuticals, this doesn't mean that as a person I am not thankful for things like vaccines, anti-biotics ect. It just means that I recognise more people tend to reach for the drug cabinet than look to the natural world and what it can supply us. We have become creatures of convenience. Of course, this is also within reason and we have to be practical here also and recognise that there are certain things we cannot cure with old folk remedies such as trying to cure cancer with half a chopped potato. Being realistic of our medical abilities helps greatly when it comes to herbology and plants. However, my disclaimer aside, that does not mean that we should turn our back upon the natural world or work with them alongside treatments we may have considered alongside the advice of a General Practitioner. We have been given this array of beautiful and healing plants and we should use them!

Sowing seeds is a great opportunity and another method for us to be able to know a plant more intimately. For instance, I've grown many different plants and herbs that I've utilised for my magical practice, and there's something special and organic about that the fact that you've literally helped give life to a plant and seen the process of its development, then to be able to utilise that within your own practice is amazing. St John's Wort plays a part in British folk magic and is an easy seed to plant as all it needs is lots of light, well-drained but also moist soil. So perhaps starting with this as a base for planting seeds may help. From personal experience, it's not been uncommon for me to have extremely vivid dreams of the seeds I have planted starting to grow, literally climbing out of the seeds and forming. The next day when I wake up, they've started to sprout. There are many grimoires and books that have had influence upon the practice of folk magic in Britain that describe and explain the secret and hidden occult virtues of plants, stones, and minerals such as the famous Sepher Raziel, Agrippa's four books of occult philosophy and Magus.

One famous book also used by cunning folk through the ages was Nicolas Culpepers complete herbal and English physician. Culpeper believed that everybody should have the right to access knowledge of medicinal herbs and plants, not just the medical elite. That the everyday people should be able to utilise their medicine in day-to-day life. The book was published in around 1652/53 and was at the time quite ground-breaking, making this knowledge more accessible to the common folk. It comes to no surprise that it was utilised by cunning people throughout the ages including James Cunning Murrell. The book also had some sections within it that were of an occult nature in the sense he categorised plants and herbs into astrological sections and even included some remedies for witchcraft such as bay leaves, wood betony, and many others.

Even from an occult point of view, to be able to go into nature and identify and harvest certain plants myself for a specific magical reason to utilise in my workings, to speak with the spirits of those plants directly, I've found incredibly useful and powerful. So be able to go outside and harvest plants for magical, food or medicinal reasons, to me gives me the feeling that not only does it make me closer to the earth; but it also honours the memories of those that have paved the way for herbal medicine and magical usage of plants such as Nicholas Culpeper.

As well as lore we have of certain plants, another aspect is that of sympathy. Meaning does the actual plant act or grow certain way or is well known for what we are wanting to conjure? In other words, it is magic based on imitation or correspondence for what we're trying to bring forth. An example of this is that we could look at the use of Privet. This well-known shrub has been used for marking boundaries between somebody's front garden and the pavement, so it acts as a boundary marker. We could work with the privet to establish boundaries between us and others. Perhaps somebody just won't get the hint or word? We could work with Privet to demonstrate those boundaries ensuring they aren't overstepped again. In fact, this shrub can even be utilised to signify a spiritual and mundane boundary within ritual and spell work. Another example of sympathia can be utilised in modern popular increase of houseplants. An example could be working with the fishbone plant or what is commonly known as a prayer plant. The leaves on these plants rise overnight and look as though they are praying, so with this in mind alongside the element of sympathetic magic, we could put a written petition buried underneath the plant. So when it prays, its constantly praying over our petition. Fishbone plants aren't native at all to the UK. However, I'm trying to demonstrate the use of sympathetic magic when it comes to plants.

Plants and their sympathetic uses aside, the following is taken from various grimoires and older herbals. The following is taken from Nicolas Culpepper's complete herbal and English physician:

Bay-*Government and virtues.*] I shall but only add a word or two to what my friend has written, *viz.*, that it is a tree of the sun, and under the celestial sign Leo, and resists witchcraft very potently, as also all the evils old Saturn can do to the body of man, and they are not a few; for it is the speech of one, and I am mistaken if it were not Mizaldus, that neither witch nor devil, thunder nor lightning, will hurt a man in the place where a Bay-tree is.

Wood Betony: "this herb is appropriated to the planet Jupiter, and the sign of Aries. Antonius Mush, physician to the emperor Agustus Caesar, wrote a peculiar book of the herb, and amongst other virtues said of it, that is preserveth the liver and body of man from the danger of epidemical diseases and from witchcraft also."

Hounds tongue: Mizaldus adds that the leaves laid under the feet, will keep the dogs from barking at you. It is called Hound's-tongue, because it ties the tongues of hounds; whether true, or not, I never tried, yet I cured the biting of a mad dog with this only medicine.

Holly: Pliny saith, the branches of the tree defend houses from lightning, and men from witchcraft.

Mistletoe: Some have so highly esteemed it for the virtues thereof, that they have called it *Lignum Sanctiæ Crucis*, Wood of the Holy Cross, believing it helps the falling sickness, apoplexy and palsy very speedily, not only to be inwardly taken, but to be hung at their neck. Separately from along side culpeppers herbal, Mistletoe is also one of the key ingredients in Medieval true love powder.

The daffodil: The first herb is known as the Daffodil is saturns and is of great efficacy in removing pains in the loins and legs. Its root parboiled, may likewise be administered with success to persons afflicted with gravel. If kept in a house where children are breeding teeth, it greatly facilitates the cutting, and assuages the pain. It banishes fear from the person who carries it about him and protects him from injury. Taken from Albertus magnus investigation of the virtues of certain herbs.

Excerpts from Sepher Raziel concerning herbs/plants

Gentian Marjoram and Valerian avail much upon great honour of princes and of great men.

Catnip alongside Marjoram, Anathanasia, clover, sage, Peruca, Ive, Artemisia, and hyssop are all joined together under a waxing moon on Jupiter's day, the next morning the sun rises from the first degree of Aries till into the first of cancer. When you gather be clean and reverent, then stand towards the east, put them on the gate of your house and you will profit forever.

A fumigation made with Linseed and Parsley will make one see into the future among other things.

Mug wort- of this herb it is said that it should be included in all that you do and whatever you wish shall come to pass, and the leaf is green on one side and white on the other and is a middling size and with this you can call and bind spirits.

Hyssop- this ought to be grown in holy places as in churches for it defends the place from evil things. It was grown by the prophets to make dead men speak that were dead for some time. In places where there is any evil he who bears this herb is able to pass freely. It gives to him might upon anything which he wishes. This herb can be placed in ana area overrun with evil and it can bind the same. Solomon said: I found in this book of Hermes, that who that takes water in the fourth hour of the night and goes upon the tomb of a dead man and mixes this herb with the water and casts it upon the tomb may communicate with the spirit therein. The water should be mixed with the juices of the herb and the person shall say:

Rise, Rise, Rise come and speak to me.

Do this for three nights and on the third he shall come and speak to you.

Rosemary- Burning the plant rosemary in the household will drive away all ill spirits and all demons. I can attest to this, as I've used this herb dried in purification and exorcism rituals of houses that have malevolent spirits dwell in them and the plant aiding within the exorcisms of people which resulted in a lot of success. an idea would be to create a bundle of rosemary to fumigate a place with, or it can be put upon hot coals and used as an incense.

Saveok Witch pits

In 2003, there was a shocking but intriguing discovery made in Saveok Cornwall. Clay pits that were approximately 42 cm long by 35 m wide and 17 cm deep, were unearthed and held within them feathers. I had the absolute pleasure of conversing with Jacqui Wood, who was one of the archaeologists who had discovered the witch pits. She had told me that the clay pits were originally found by accident, as archaeologists were excavating a Mesolithic clay platform and found the pits that ran into it. Initially archaeologists claimed that they may have been used for plucking. A practice that was common in the turn of the century. However, upon further inspection, there was a discovery that the feathers were attached to skin and that the pelt of a bird was buried in these pits.

When taking them to a zoo for further inspection, they discovered the bird utilised was a swan. Another find during the inspection of this pit was small stones, which seemed to be wrapped in organic matter such as leaves, and bird claws included from different types of birds. What was then discovered was that the stones came from fifteen miles down the river from the original site. The grisly discovery soon escalated, and more and more pits were discovered again holding within them swan pelts but also more gruesome finds such as the corpses of 2 dead magpies buried either side. An even more sinister discovery was made when there were 55 eggs inputted into this pit, in which 7 found that were just about to hatch that had been buried in these pits preserving their membranes. The carbon dating ranged from 1640, to wait for it, 1970s. Meaning there still may be somebody alive today who would have performed this ritual. There were other items found within these pits, at one point a cat, a dog, and a goat that had been buried and preserved in these mysterious pits. Overall, there were over 50 witch pits discovered from different time periods.

Nobody knows for sure what these pits were used for, but an interesting factor here was that some were seen to have had the contents of them taken out. Archaeologists speculated that perhaps they were used as a fertility ritual in the sense that if you become with child, the contents would be taken out burning the body of the swan thus setting its spirit free as the swan is associated with St Brigid. However, if you didn't become with child, you left the contents therein. Another factor here is that in some charms of British folk magic, St Brigid is seen as the midwife for the virgin mother who helped delivered Jesus. This again reiterates the narrative of her association with fertility and midwifery. What's so fascinating to me is the fact that when asking other sources such as the museum of witchcraft in Boscastle, there was no known ritual of the sort. It's also interesting again that these pits are dated at different times and periods in history. So whoever has been carrying this on and doing such a ritual act has kept this very secretive indeed.

Witch Pit: a modern rite.

With all this information given, I wanted to present a modern variation of this and one that doesn't involve mercilessly killing a poor defenceless animal. In good humour, I'd be obliged to call it a 'vegetarian version'. Dig a hole deep enough to input the contents. Then is your time to petition St Brighid. There are different ways to do this, but I would have a paper image of her printed out and make this the first item to lay within the pit asking for her blessing.

A way to do this is the lay the image down in the empty pit, repeating her prayer:

St Brighid you were a voice for the wounded and the wary. Strengthen what is weak within us, calm us into a quietness that heals and listens, may we grow each day into greater wholeness in mind body and spirit

At this moment, commune with St Brighid and literally pour your heart out, tell her your desire and need to have a child and why you want a child in your life. Literally speak from the depths of your heart really taking your time, as twee as that may sound, speak directly from your heart. After this has been done finish the prayer off by saying: *AMEN.* Now what needs to then be put into the pit are the feathers of swans, as well as many different other birds making sure they are gathered ethically, whilst nothing is harmed gathering these items. Use these feathers to line the pits.

Then add into the hole, eggs bought from the supermarket. Add hen eggs, duck eggs, quail eggs, the more variety the better. Making sure these eggs don't break in the pit, start to carefully place them at the bottom. The next items are seeds. Remember the discovered witch pits contained different animals found within them, emblematic of the term: a life for a life. Seeds are still life, if we are to be granted a new life then we must give up another life in order to achieve this. Seeds do this in a way that doesn't cause suffering. Then oats are sprinkled into the pit representing fertility and fecundity. Other items can be added such as old birds' nest that are no longer used if found, making sure they're not still in use. Lastly, sexual fluids from the woman and man desiring to have a child are mixed together and poured into the pit. If the couple are same sex for men, it will be a mix of both their semen, for women their menstrual blood or sexual fluids. If it is for a woman alone, then her sexual fluids or menstrual blood will suffice.

Again, this imitates the life for a life element here. Once all this has been put into the pit, then start to bury it. After you've finished burying the items of power in the pit, take some whole milk or cream, and state the prayer to Brigid again as mentioned previously. Do it in exactly the same manner as you did concerning opening your heart. Once that's been done, give the cream over the buried pit as an offering to the spirits, walk away and don't look back. Once you have become with child, then you are to go back to the pit and dig the contents up once more, unearthing as much as possible and giving thanks to the spirits for their help.

The Power of the written word

Another element of British folk magic is the power of the written word, and its influences within magical history. Some of these in a sense were written like letters for a variety of petitions, often containing names of God that weren't particularly spoken in verses but were morely written down such as the word AGLA (meaning You oh Lord are mighty forever) carrying the idea of the power of the name of divinity when written down. Various examples of these written talismans are contained within this book from dispersing vapours, to protecting the homestead from hauntings. Another two examples, are firstly a letter that was found concealed in a farm in Lancashire, bearing protective symbols and written statements to protect and defend against the measures and influence of the black witch. Another example is the use of a letter found in the grimoire of Arthur gauntlet (Rankine) (Sloane MS3851) which protects those against all harm, and is to be carried around as a way to protect the person from all harm. This also vibrates the understanding of the social aspect that were occurring at these points in time.

During the early modern period, literacy amongst the working class was a rarity and only around a small number of people were literate. The ability to read and write in some ways was seen as a gift and seen that the person exerted some knowledge and power. In fact, it wasn't uncommon for cunning folk to have books but to not actually have the ability to read. This may sound ridiculous but to their clients at the time, it would have looked impressive, nevertheless. With this element in mind, an idea could be for those to utilise the power of the written word as amulets and talismans. Once again, to help bring particular influences such as health, anti-theft, anti-witchcraft, protection from danger/accidents, ect.

I have supplied a couple of examples here involving these pieces of written folk magic that can be utilized and worked upon. An idea as a way to bless these charms could be to fumigate them in specific herbs/resins that carry those vibrations you wish to draw. So, for example, one could use a fumigation combination of wood betony, bay and St john's wort as a way to deter any maleficia or ill-will being sent to them. For the curing of ailemtns, also aspersing them with Holy water or water collected from various wells or Holy Springs that have a reputation for curing ailments or any other healing required.

Letter 1: For Finance. To be constructed on the day of Jupiter, In the hour of Jupiter, bearing the seal of Jupiter underneath it. Fumigated in Marigold, ginger, anise, and juniper berries.

"The Lord Elab hear my call and supplication, In the name of Jophiel, your generous hand is open and flows freely rewarding those who are worthy of the rich fruits of this earth, the overshadowing of Poverty will not darken me, for with you Lord, the light of your generosity will shine in my face forever as your hand flows freely. Money before me, money behind me, money to the right of me, Money to the left of me. Et nomine et patri et filli et spiritus sanctum FIAT FIAT FIAT AMEN!"

Letter 2: Against Knife Crime

"Our Lord Christ was speared through his side by the Romans and yet still he was immortalized by the Power of Adonai. I call upon you O lord, who is mighty forever, that no spear shall penetrate me, no blade shall touch me, no knife shall wound me, no weapon shall cut me. The lord will keep me safe and preserve me from all violence, from all wounds, from all knives, In his name I shall be saved in his name I give my trust, and from his trust all blades shall break and shatter in his power and my skin shall be as Iron. FIAT FIAT FIAT!!!

An interesting section in witchcraft detected and prevented features written petitions to be carried about a person for different amounts of purposes. This also combines elements of astrology, which calls upon the powers and virtues of planets and star signs. I have included a handful of the following here:

These misfortunes generally happen under the power of the moon. Who (as ancients hold) is the one who favours of magic or enchantment take the opposite planet to her in a line her force this way which is Jupiter? Write his character loss of this planet on a piece of parchment and add to it the following characters that are the signs of the zodiac namely for Virgo Aquarius Scorpio these numbers 1, 3, 2, 5, 7, 1-1,1-7,1-4th: after this sat down the number of the figurative letters in your name make, wrap it up in a smaller compass as you can, and sewing it up in a piece of black silk that has been steeped in juice of vervain comma hang it about your neck when the moon changes and you will be sure from any danger of this nature if you lead a good life.

The following written charm again from witchcraft detected and prevented features a safeguard for an orchard, park, woodlot, or field. Unfortunately, in this modern-day nature reserves and natural areas are ever more threatened by the presence of human consumption and greed. Particularly when it comes to spaces or places in which the folk magician will work. This charms me radiates one of the many ways we As folk magicians can protect natural landscapes around us.

A safeguard for an orchard, park, woodlands, or field.

The several places being guarded by one and the same planet, not to be too tedious to you, one and the same thing will in differently serve to secure any of them from the thieves that come to make robbery or depredation comma whether it be for fruits of the earth or any kind of cattle, or to steal away timber in fields or Woods; to make witch, take the following direction, have a piece of curious clean parchment, made of a sleek skin, cut it with 5 points or corners in the form of a star, but so large that you may write in the centre of it, what is to be written, mainly, Libra, Sagittarius, Pisces, the characters of the celestial signs governed in these affairs, add the character of the planet for the day, as before directed, and suppose it to be Tuesday, Mars that govern that day has a character, then write: 1,7,11,12,1-2,1-8th. Closer top with virgins wax, as I should have told you, (you ought to have done with the former and sprinkle it with the juice of fumitory and place it in the same if in a garden in a hole of a wall.) If in a forest, park, or woods, in the hole of a tree, having laid it before induced tansy and so forth. whatsoever any thief takes in these several grounds, he shall not be able to carry off till the sunrise in but then if not watched he may do it.

    Another interesting piece taken from the Liber Solomonis: Sepher Raziel speaks of the use of Holy names of God in order to achieve various outcomes:

Johac, Jona, Eloy, Yena.
Know that whoever has these names upon parchment, that in Hebrew is named Genilin guided letters with him or on his clothing, will lack nothing.

Mari Berllan Bitter's Charm

Born in 1817 in the parish of Llanddewi Aberarth Wales, Mari Berllan Bitter was a woman who was said by the locals to be a fierce witch whose reputation would cripple the community around her in fear. She would be seen going around local farms in Cardiganshire carrying an empty basket on her arm. It was said farmers who refused to give the woman any food would find their milk curdled or their cattle dead the following day. I have an account and charm here that is from a man who remembers Mari as a child. Unfortunately and admittedly in terms of referencing this information its not from a book. I came across this in a BBC program known as Celtic Monsters: Witches:

> The best-known Welsh witch in recent times was known as Mari Berllan Bitter. This is a story told by Daniel Herbert in 1979 when he was in his 90s, as a child he lived on the next farm to Mari in Pontrhydfendigaid and this is his account:
>
> *"My first memory of Mari is when I was about 2 or 3 years old. My mother used to run errands for her getting her bread, sugar, and tea things like that and my sister and I would take them down to Berllan Pitter. She was a tiny old lady always with a shawl over her shoulders and a hat covering her head, I remember us visiting once and going over to sit on the settle. Mari was sitting on the corner and there was a pile of autumn leaves in front of*

the fire blown in from outside, suddenly we saw the leaves moving and we were so frightened we drew our legs up. Mari got up and just bent down and grabbed the snake out of the leaves and then she put it in her blouse. That's where she kept it, the snake lived in the house with her. She certainly had an influence over you, we used to tell her everything and one day we asked her how she cast her spells. "I'll tell you "She said. You see that basin of water over there on my table, my ball of wool, I put the ball of wool in the water I go to the bible, and I read a particular chapter, and that's when I noticed, her ball of wool was full of pins. She died in 1898 and we saw the coffin coming out of the house. John her cousin was there together with the mayor that she said to have witched. They put the coffin in the trap and John shouted: Lets go Bess she won't witch you today, she's quiet enough now. No one ever lived at Berllan Pitters home after that."

-Script provided by readable

One of the reasons I am suppling Mari's charm, is because I have worked this particular charm myself. There are so many passages in the bible that can be read out as a mantra or chant, focusing on the intent literally driving your intention into something. This charm I used has worked too well, so what I will say is from my own personal experience, please approach this one with caution. I've also wanted to input this charm into this book, as it keeps the memory of Mari Berllan Bitter alive and preserves her work and practice.

On Witch Bottles for a myriad of other uses rather than magical contagion and apotropaic manners.

The famous witch bottle is an object that has become well known when it comes to British folk magic and has appeared in various other countries and folk magic traditions over the years. Its use as mentioned earlier in this book, primarily have been centred around the idea of magical contagion. The bottle itself acting as a spiritual decoy so that any maleficia sent by ill wishing witches or the evil eye, would attach itself to the bottle rather than the intended target. Sometimes it was created to be destroyed in order to send back any evil that had befallen the one who had been bewitched. However apotropaic uses aside, the witch bottle isn't just limited to this.

It can have a myriad of spiritual uses and within my own praxis, I have used this bottle to conjure forth various desires ranging from finance, health to even gaining a new flatmate. It becomes within itself a holding vessel for the power and intentions set. In a nutshell, the bottle has various items put inside it that represent the different things you're wanting to conjure. For instance if it were for finding a new flatmate, the bottle would have plants associated with money on it so that they were a person who could pay their bills on time, daisies for a good friendship, perhaps a statement of intention declaring your need for a new flat mate, psalms with corresponding statements of what you're desiring. In essence, the list could go on. Iron for strength, vinegar for cursing work or making somebodies life bitter, violets for love or romance, sugar to sweeten somebody's intentions etc. There are really no rules to this, it's entirely something of your own creation. I find this kind of practice exciting as it gives you a chance to make it yours. With each item added into the bottle, words are muttered representing what you're trying to draw towards you or a targeted person. So again, in the instance of gaining a new flatmate, using sugar one may say:

By sugar may their intentions be always sweet towards me and towards the property

The same is done again with adding dust that been swept up and gathered in the flat:

By the dust of this place, may they be suited for this flat and be good for this property

This again is just an example, but I think when it comes to this it is just a way of showing you that the sky is the limit here to what you can add. Each item can be spoken to, and intention is put into the item to bring about your desire. As each item is added, the practitioner can work up an ongoing and trance inducing chant tailored towards what they want. Personally, for me, I am a fan of inducing trance through a chant whilst intently visualising what I want coming to fruition. In terms of what chant to utter in your conjurations, I tend to find the more simplistic the better for example:

New flatmate, new flatmate, new flatmate to me.

If you're a fan of religious use in your practice, then you could add a bible passage or sentences that corresponds to your desired outcome. Afterwards, a candle is to be placed into the neck of the bottle and lit with a statement of intention:

Hear my words and hear them well, by my will I light this candle to bring a new flatmate to 77 sirens way, Milton drive by sugar they will be a sweet person, by rosemary and chamomile, they will be financially secure, by daisy chain they will become a good friend, spirits bring about this will and bless it.

After everything has been listed what resides in the bottle state the words strongly:

FIAT FIAT FIAT!!!

Keep the bottle somewhere safe until what you desire comes to light. If, however in the instance of directing the bottle towards a specific person, hide the bottle near their property so that they come into regular contact with the vessel.

The witches swing

Cecil Williamson claimed that one of the first conjurations he worked, was given to him by a school nurse, who also happened to be an avid practitioner of the black arts. At the time, he suffered the abuse of a bully in his school, and he was instructed to work a charm. The conjuration was in essence to build a swing on a tree, to light a fire, and then to put a handful of grass on the fire causing it to smoke. As the fire smoked, he swung through this to and fro chanting repetitively: *"Bullstrode away, Bullstrode away."* After the school holidays had passed, Cecil had claimed that Bullstrode the troublesome and notorious school bully did not appear at school again and had suffered a horrific skiing incident. The repetitive act of going back and forth on a swing, working yourself into a deep trance and chanting the desired outcome as you pass through the rising smoke, seems to make perfect sense to me as a practitioner of folk magic.

From a magical perspective, I can completely see how this would work. I can attest that I have gone into heavy and deep trances whilst on a swing watching the moonlit sky bathing the land in its essence. It wasn't an actual intentional thing too, just post ritual fun with a good friend of mine with whom ive had the pleasure of working with magically over the years Jonathan Pheonix-Archer. Yes, I understand I am in my thirties and yes life is too bloody short to not get on a swing and reclaim that inner child every once in a while! Live your best life is a regular saying of mine. Of course, from a magical perspective making your own swing would be effective because of the input and energy that goes into that. However, for the magician in the city this would be a hard and difficult thing to do.

So, an idea would be to utilise the use of an ordinary swing whilst keeping the chant simplistic and as straightforward as Cecil did. Instead of building a bonfire, (in which I can't imagine you being very popular risking burning down a children's playground) perhaps having a vessel with a lit charcoal inside and a blend of incense from your own making, charged with your intent for your specific desire. So, for instance perhaps for a new job a mix of fenugreek, clover, valerian, heather, and cinnamon. With an easy and simplistic statement of intention like Cecil used. As the practitioner swings to and fro, keeping their intent set on the desired outcome passing through the rising smoke and working a chant such as: "new job, new job, come to me."

I don't see why this method alongside the conjuration would not work. However, PLEASE beware because swinging through a fiery vessel of incense back and forth during the daytime, as well as talking to yourself where children play frequently, wouldn't be a good look and would incur the chance of little Timmy genuinely being traumatised thinking somebody is practicing satanism on his swing. I mean it goes without saying too that night-time really is best for this working

To gain influence over a place

A very simplistic and effective way at gaining your influence over a certain place be it home, work, another

person's threshold etc. Is to gather and take the dirt from outside that place and to carry it home with you. This working really is versatile in the sense the intentions can be set up for any place, and really has no limit to what intentions you set. They can be for good or for ill. It could be for influencing a workplace making you more seen and noticed for that job promotion you've been wanting for a while. It could be for cursing or bewitching another's household, to bring money into your own home, the list really does go on. To begin this simplistic conjuration, gather the dirt from the place you're wanting influence. Take the dirt in a bowl, placing your hands over the vessel whilst pushing energy into the dirt, visualising, and seeing your goal happening repeatedly. Really take your time in pushing those intentions into the dirt from your hands, seeing your desires manifesting. At this point you can even ask any familiar spirits you work with to also help bless the dirt with your intentions. Then take the vessel up, and speak loudly to it words of your choice for example:

"Hear my words, from this point on you will hold influence over my workplace. I shall hold the power, I shall hold influence, I shall be more respected ect."

At this point after the conjuration is said, take the vessel and breath into it your intention. Another option is a long yawning exhale, literally breathing in your intentions. This is to breathe life into the dirt, to give your intentions and your will life so that it will take power in the threshold.

Yawning was also a popular practice utilised by some cunning folk in Scotland and is mentioned in the book Witchcraft and the second sight in the highlands and islands of Scotland by John Gregorson Campbell. It is taken from an account of a wisewoman yawning upon some water in order to combat the evil eye. After the yawning or breathing of intent, take a small candle (small birthday candles work best) leaving it in the middle of the vessel and light it. Leave it until the following morning, then your dirt is ready to be re-scattered back to its original place, to work your will and influence. You caN even scatter it into a place of work rather than outside if circumstances permit.

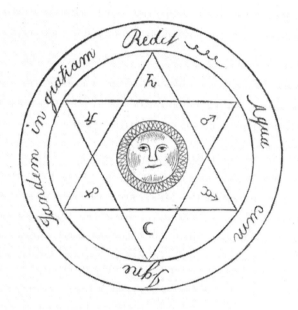

Image taken from the book the wonderfull discoverie in the countie of Lancaster by Thomas Potts published in 1613. The Image was inscripted onto Websters monument in the Chapel of St Mary magdalen Clitheroe, which was described as 'too characteristic and curious to be omitted'. The place was described in the book as 'Wizard haunted'.

Conclusion

From the early modern period up until now, there has been huge significant numerous changes in terms of our surroundings, our innovations, technology, social attitudes, Healthcare, and communications. The access we now have now to tackle a varied amount of health problems ranges, whether it be the ability to kill warts off with medical home kits, or the ability to have access to medicine. In reference to some of the charms mentioned in this book are based around rural and agricultural settings, many of us are not farmers and don't have cattle. In fact, a lot of people tend to live and work within the cities. We now also have access to food a lot more easily, than those opposed to the early modern period.

Another aspect of this being the progression of medicine and vaccinations. Thus warding away illnesses such as the flu, typhoid, polio, the plague, ect. Thankfully, we now in modern day Britain, have access to things that are quite literally able to save our lives. So what comes with these innovations, and what does the access we now have mean for folk magic? It means that older and sundry remedies for curing warts, curing diseases, cattle charming, cease to be as people are now able to find more quick and efficient ways to tackle these problems. The trouble with this is that because of this, it then allows folk magic to become lost as a tradition and art. This especially during the present day, where things in general have now become so disposable.

A large majority of people today in my opinion, have lost their way. They don't know much about their own history, heritage, folklore, and culture. They have become completely ensnared and engulfed in technology, head down, unable to see when the next car is pulling up and nearly getting themselves run over, let alone paying awareness to elements of previous magical practice. They have become so out of touch, and are able to quickly identify brand labels but cannot identify trees and plants. This isn't to say all people have become this but a large majority of people, have become so out of touch with the real world around them. Only having a consideration in regard to the next selfie or picture they take that they're able to upload to a social media platform. Stories of spirits and faeries start to raise more eyebrows complete with side eye sniggering, older tales of lore of the land slowly starts to disappear back into the land. As people walk around ensnared by technology, unable to look up around them whilst the very landscape around them is being destroyed and impacted for corporate greed.

Now I'm sure this all sounds depressing and believe me, I'm not wanting you to finish this book on an all-time low. It's just that I feel to help preserve British folk magic, we must be mindful of the times we're now in and what we're now facing in terms of disassociation. However, people being as now cut off as ever (in my opinion) doesn't change the fact that around every corner deep down on a primitive level in each person, the belief in contagion and magic still very much exists. There was a study done on a television program by Professor Ronald Hutton called Britain's Wicca man; an interesting documentary on the envelopment and creation of the religion/practice of Wicca. During this documentary, it featured an experiment between a group of psychology students where they were told to stab a photograph of a loved one with a knife. Even the most sceptical of people could not go ahead and do this, just incase 'something happened'.

There are also things that have become embedded into each person. For instance, when they speak of something bad, they'll 'knock on wood' or 'touch wood' for luck that anything negative doesn't befall themselves or a loved on which their speaking of. Horseshoes are still hung up over doors, as people are aware they are used as 'lucky' or 'protective' to ward away any evil befalling the household. These are things that people still observe to this day and of course, British folk magic still carries on currently as there are those that are still contacted for helping cure cattle or ward away any illness particularly within rural workers and farmers.

However, for these traditions to survive, they must be practiced and move with the modern times. So, what are we able to do to help British folk magic survive? Maybe go with the times but retain that essence of connection to the natural world that many others are missing. Perhaps utilise the modern world with what we have around us. For instance, if somebody is burnt and they run their hand underneath a cold running tap, then reciting a burn charm over that with the aid of the cold water would go hand in hand to help heal the burn? Perhaps we could try and charm the wart away before reaching for the bazooka? or perhaps we could even offer our services as healers if we see somebody has fallen ill on social media? Not only does it help preserve folk magic in general but above all, it's just kind. I have charmed people in multiple places and circumstances such as social media platforms, house parties, and during work. All these things work hand in hand with older folk charms and cures. I still, to this day will rather reach for the herb cabinet than jumping for the medicine cabinet any day.

Let me be perfectly clear though its not say I don't use medicine, of course I do. I just think its important to try natural approaches first. There have also been times where the charming I have performed has left those in medical fields absolutely baffled. For instance, the spell included in this book for those with breathing problems was originally worked upon a beloved pet of mine Dylan who was a bearded dragon. Each time she has a coughing attack, I would put her in the bath and work the same charm upon her. It was thought at first, she has respiratory lung infection which unfortunately is found within lizards and snakes. Though sadly, it was much bigger and uglier than that. When she had a scan, she had actually passed away however what was actually found is that she had Tuberculosis. The veterinary surgeon was genuinely bewildered as to why she was still alive and said at this point she should have already been dead at least a year ago. I didn't mention to him what I had done as I think there can be a line of ego sometimes which I'd hate to arise, and ive seen ego get extremely ugly in some practitioners and I didn't want to radiate that. I just said she had a strong spirit. Which was not a lie, she really did.

A charm I can recall of utilising older folk magical practices within the modern day, is a witch bottle I made to get a flatmate. Myself and my previous partner at the time, had a flatmate leave our flat and we had to find one soon. Money at the time was at a limit and reluctantly, we were forced to put an advert up online advertising the apartment and room. This was something we were both wary of, as I have heard a lot of horror stories and the idea of recruiting a stranger online felt a bit scary. Because of this very reason, I decided to employ magic as a way for us to find a suitable flatmate. After a couple of days later, I had put the advertisement up and I received a call from a man, strangely recognising the voice that was speaking back to me on the phone. We carried on speaking about the apartment and then he paused for a second and said: "Wait a minute.... Your George aren't you?" "You've got a partner called Josh? Its John from the gym!" The person that rang me was at the time a gym instructor from a gym I frequently went to, and I had chatted to him quite a lot. Seven years on, and we were still living together!

What's important is that at this point, we do not allow the modern world to swallow up our history and these acts of spiritual healing, instead we work with it. There are still countries that hold folk magical healing close to them such as Belarus just outside of Poland. Which has its whispering witches who prefer to be called whisperers rather than witches, but tend to still be consulted to this day by a myriad of old and young people alike. The trouble is this practice is dying out, as those that are younger are moving out of Belarus area as there is little opportunity for them and much more opportunities in bigger cities. So with that, the next generation of whisperers is ever so quickly depleting. In Ireland, shockingly to my surprise I have had conversations with nineteen-year-olds in Dublin city centre in a club of all places about their local folklore.

They were telling me of older superstitions and folk tales about the little people and their characteristics. What they knew about their own history and folklore was truly inspiring to see compared to younger British people. Who most of the time, are the opposite way in the sense they know very little about their own history and folklore.

By us performing older charms and spells that are based off older practices, in the modern day it helps keep the memories of these charms alive. A truly beautiful thought that arises whenever I perform certain historical charms or spells, is that at that very moment of performing the rite, I stop being George and start becoming that ritual that has been done by many different people over a myriad of time periods. That in itself is keeping the praxis of folk magic alive. Many results that can be had by these conjurations and sundry charms can really affect people and tend to in my experiences, stay with them to the day they die. I have known people that are folk magicians that have been in relationships with those who are sceptical Catholics, who then have stories to tell in regard to what has occurred through their partners charming them or their friends. Work colleagues that will never forget how strange it was that a spell somebody performed for them worked. They then go on to tell others about their experiences, stories like this often tend to start with: "This may seem crazy but!" By these stories being told, they then are preserved and immortalised, showing that a normal modern-day individual had a run in with a charmer or a witch that was able to cure their toothache, or their cold, or any other problems they have. Those stories then pass on and keep the memory of folk magical healing alive, it keeps the blood pumping around its heart and slowly but surely starts to re-enchant people and the world around it. Bringing back that belief in magic that deep down on a primitive level, still exists within all humans. I have known people that practice folk magic to utilise their charms on people they have seen in the streets who have had accidents whilst they are waiting for the ambulance, and this has been done from what they have said with great affect.

There are also news reports of people that are able to charm and contacted by different clients, such as a BBC news report on a woman named Rebecca Hamilton who lives in Donegal Ireland who has the gift of what she calls 'the cure'. With this gift, she charms a variety of ailments such as ringworm, shingles, mouth ulcers, cold sores, and curing off for sheep which she says is unusual, but she just says the prayers for the person that owns the sheep and that seems to work. She receives calls from all over the world and charms also over the phone, asking for people's names reciting them in her secretive prayers. Over the past 40 years, she has claimed to have helped thousands of people with her gift. Admittedly, I had originally come about this story online and even in the comments section, there were many people asking for her contact number as they wanted to get in touch with her so that she would be able to cure them of any ailments that they had. Moments like this in our modern world, reiterate just how much the human condition believes in the magic of sympathethia, magical symbolism, faith, and contagion.

This shows more than anything that with our connection now have to others in the modern world, that we can use all of this to our advantage and utilise the power of communication to reach out to others and to allow others to reach out to us and provide any magical services others may desire. Rather than seeing the modern world as an obstacle to our practice, we can utilise this! In writing all this and in contrast to what has been said, I hope the introduction to this conclusion has not depressed you too much! As I want to show examples of aspects of the modern world that risk these older practices, but then to also show how we are then able to work along-side the modern world as I feel this is important to help preserve these traditions.

    I sincerely hope that this book has given you the information, tools, and examples utilised to build and help structure your own personal folk magical practice. Sometimes one of the things I feel that can lack from books centred around modern magical folk practice, is the ability to list references and show people where certain charms and spells originate from. This I feel is important as it credits the working people/cunning folk/witches that have shared them through different points in history and allows them to have memory and live on through the legacy left behind. I also wanted to make it understandable too as I know not everybody can interpret some academic linguistics well, in which isn't an attack at all upon those books that utilise such language. I have the upmost respect for those that do, I'm just wanting to make this book more relatable for everyone.

    I think that with the conclusion please know by practicing British folk magic, it doesn't make you the same as a cunning man or wisewoman from the early modern period. Those were extremely different times and cunning folk served their local community, where many had completely different mind frames and mindsets entirely. Another aspect is the fact that these times were completely different, in terms of others' views of the world around them and the firm belief in the supernatural. So please bare this in mind. I just wanted to make the material herein accessible to everybody as I know there are people that struggle sometimes with this specific style of referencing. As a practitioner, I have so much respect for people that do publish books on the matter especially books on spells, charms, incantations of British folk magic as I feel by British folk magic being written down and being made accessible to the people, it preserves it as a practice and carries on its survival. It helps carry on those older customs and traditions that are sadly unknown and lost to a large proportion of Brits today. I hope that reading by this book, I have done exactly what ive set out to accomplish and inspire you within your own practice bringing magic to your life and hopefully immortalizing and progressing the praxis of modern British folk magic.

Recommended reading and Bibliography

Agrippa, Cornelius, *Agrippa four books of occult philosophy.* 1531

Anonymous, *The black pullet.* 1740

Baker, Jim, *The cunning man's handbook.* 2014

Barett Fraancis, *The Magus.* 1801

Campbell, Gregorson, *witchcraft and second sight in the highlands and islands of Scotland.* 1902

Davies, Owen,*Popular magic.* 2003

Dörfler, Peter, *Albertus Magnus: Being the Approved, Verified, Sympathetic and Natural Egyptian Secrets : White and Black Art for Man and Beast : the Book of Nature and the Hidden Secrets and Mysteries of Life Unveiled.* 1919

Froome,, Joyce, *Wicked enchantments a history of the pendle witches and their magic.* 2012

Gary, Gemma, *The black toad.* 2012

Gary, Gemma, *Traditional witchcraft a Cornish book of ways.* 2008

Howard, Michael, *East Anglian witches and wizards.* 2017

King, Graham, *The British book of charms and spells.* 2016

Mercer, Andrew, *The wicked shall decay.* 2018

Mills, Ash William, *The Black book of Isobel Gowdie and other Scottish & Charms.* 2021

Nostradamus, Gabriel, *Consult the oracle: a Victorian guide to folklore and fortune telling.* 2013

Rankine, David.ed, *The grimoire of Arthur gauntlet: a seventeenth century London cunning man's book of charms conjurations and prayers.* 2011

Scot, Reginald, *The discoverie of witchcraft.* 1584

Singer, William, *an exposition on the Miller and Horseman's word or the true system of raising the devil* 1881

Wilby, Emma, *Cunning folk and familiar spirits.* 2002

About the author

George Hares is a practicing Witch, British folk magician, and root worker located in Edinburgh Scotland. He has been practicing and researching folk magic in its various forms for over 20 years. Originally born in native 'witch country' Essex, he enjoys creating videos for his YouTube channel George Hares which focuses on the magical arts particularly within the traditions of British folk magic and traditional witchcraft. He is also an avid tarot reader who like witchcraft has been practicing since he was 11. Originally a trained dancer, he enjoys taking contemporary dance lessons, as well as lifting weights in the gym.

Find him on You tube: George Hares

Instagram: thenorthenglishwitch